Location-Based Marketing

FOR ~~DUMMIES~~®

Jodi ♡

You're no Dummy

but thanks for your
support! Means a lot
to have you as a friend!

Mike

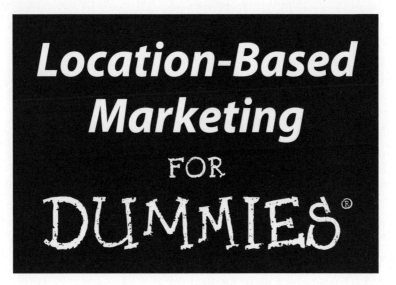

Location-Based Marketing

FOR

DUMMIES®

by **Aaron Strout and Mike Schneider**

Foreword by BJ Emerson
VP Technology, Tasti D-Lite

WILEY

John Wiley & Sons, Inc.

Location-Based Marketing For Dummies®

Published by
John Wiley & Sons, Inc.
111 River Street
Hoboken, NJ 07030-5774
www.wiley.com

For general information on our other products and services, please contact our Customer Care Department within the U.S. at 877-762-2974, outside the U.S. at 317-572-3993, or fax 317-572-4002.

For technical support, please visit www.wiley.com/techsupport.

Wiley also publishes its books in a variety of electronic formats and by print-on-demand. Not all content that is available in standard print versions of this book may appear or be packaged in all book formats. If you have purchased a version of this book that did not include media that is referenced by or accompanies a standard print version, you may request this media by visiting http://booksupport.wiley.com. For more information about Wiley products, visit us www.wiley.com.

Library of Congress Control Number: 2011935394

ISBN 978-1-118-02249-8 (pbk); ISBN 978-1-118-13204-3 (ebk); ISBN 978-1-118-13205-0 (ebk); ISBN 978-1-118-13206-7 (ebk)

Manufactured in the United States of America

10 9 8 7 6 5 4 3 2 1

WILEY

About the Authors

Aaron Strout is the head of location-based marketing at WCG, a global agency offering integrated creative, interactive, and marketing communications services to clients in healthcare, consumer products, and technology. At WCG, Aaron not only focuses on helping customers with mobile location-based marketing and social media but also helps provide a social voice for the company.

In his current role, Aaron is a frequent speaker and blogger, podcaster, and social networker. Prior to joining WCG, Aaron spent time as the CMO of social media agency Powered Inc., VP of social media at Mzinga, and director of interactive at Fidelity Investments.

In addition to his knowledge of the interactive and social media landscape, Aaron has more than 17 years of online marketing and advertising experience, with a strong background in integrated and online marketing. Aaron is a founding member and former president of Boston Interactive Media Association (BIMA) and a member and former board member of the Massachusetts Innovation & Technology Exchange (MITX).

Mike Schneider is Senior Vice President and Director Digital Incubator for Allen & Gerritsen, ranked by Advertising Age as one of the Top 50 independent advertising agencies in the U.S. The DInc is an emerging technology lab responsible for building products and engaging digital experiences rooted in ROI while helping define "what's next" for the agency and the industry.

Mike has spent his career solving problems using technology with a focus on marketing and analytics. He began his career building enterprise-class, database-driven applications and data warehouses. Opportunities to get his hands on world-class technology projects and management consulting opportunities brought him to organizations like Ernst & Young and Oracle. In 2004, he took his CRM and analytics expertise to Hill Holliday where he built the database marketing practice and also ran the digital technology practice. His client roster includes: Cognos, CVS, Dunkin' Donuts, Fidelity Investments, Dell, Gillette, Georgia Pacific, Hannaford, Liberty Mutual, LPL, MFS, Murphy USA, Pfizer, Sears, Spike TV, xFinity, and WBUR.

Mike has crafted paid-, owned-, and earned-media strategies, built award-winning communities, and designed and implemented location-based, customer segmentation, content management, and customer relationship management solutions. He also writes for several blogs, including a technology and social media blog called Digital Before Digital. He was recognized in 2010 as a *Boston Business Journal* 40 Under 40 honoree. He is the host of a web show called Tech Interruption (http://techinterruption.com).

Authors' Acknowledgments

Aaron Strout: They aren't kidding when they say writing a book is hard. But as the old adage goes, "what doesn't kill you can only make you stronger." Boy, do I feel strong.

In completing this book, it is a good feeling to be able to look back and thank all of the people that made it possible. That list certainly starts with my beautiful and loving wife, Melanie, and continues right on through to my three wonderful children, Olivia, Benjamin, and Audrey, who may have thought it was cool when I first told them I was writing a book but by the end of the process were quite unimpressed. I'd also like to share the love with my mom and dad who did a bang-up job of raising me and taught me right from wrong, and to my brother John and sister Heather, who are as good a pair of siblings as one could ask for.

Then there are all the people that made this book what it is. First up is our acquiring editor at Wiley, Amy Fandrei. Without her, Mike and I would never have been asked to submit a book proposal. Equally important is our taskmaster/mentor/muse, Rebecca Senninger — also known as our project editor. Last but not least are Heidi Unger and Chris Banks, our copy and technical editors. This team collectively pushed us to create a better book.

Let's not forget to thank our foreword author, BJ Emerson. Not only did he do a fantastic job kicking this book off, but he is also one of the reasons Mike and I got into the LBS space in the first place. And then there are the men and women at the companies that make location-based services happen: foursquare, Gowalla, SCVNGR, WHERE, Whrrl (now Groupon), Bizzy, MomentFeed, and Geotoko. Yes, this means you Dennis Crowley, Naveen Selvardurai, Tristan Walker, Eric Friedman, Josh Williams, Andy Ellwood, Pia Burone, Jeff Holden, Heather Meeker, Seth Priebatsch, Chris Mahl, Rob Reed, Adarsh Pallian, Ryan Kuder, Natalie Kogan, and many of the other LBS masters.

Additional thanks go to the folks at Ben & Jerry's, Chris Baccus at AT&T, Cyriac Roeding at shopkick, Asif Kahn and his fantastic organization Location Based Marketing Association (LBMA), Simon Salt of IncSlingers for his insight and introductions, Scott Hampson, a.k.a. Agent-X for his awesome Batman cartoon (`www.agent-x.com.au`), the folks at eMarketer, Kris Duggan at Badgeville, and fellow LBS enthusiasts Jason Keath, Wayne Sutton, Jill McFarland, Tim Hayden, Walter Elly, and Eric Andersen.

Let's not forget the kind gentlemen at WCG — my current workplace — Jim Weiss and Bob Pearson, who egged me on and supported me every step of the way. I also would be remiss if I left out Ken Nicolson, my friend and mentor at my former employer, Powered, along with my friend and three-time author,

Joseph Jaffe (what has two thumbs, speaks a little bit of French . . .). Also thanks to Barry Libert who taught me a heck of a lot of things about thought leadership; my good friend Jim Storer who schooled me on blogging and community management; my podcast partners Kyle Flaherty, Jennifer Leggio, and Greg Matthews, who I forced to talk about location-based services more than they would have liked; and friends/smarties like Chris Brogan, Bryan Person, and Doug Haslam who experimented with me back in 2007 on Brightkite. Oh, and Andy Kaufman for turning me on to foursquare in early 2009, and Jeremiah Owyang, Francois Gossieaux, Rick Calvert, and Mukund Mohan for believing in me starting back in 2007.

Last but not least, I'd like to thank my coauthor, partner in crime, brother in arms, and favorite imitator of Borat, @SchneiderMike. I'd call him by his real name, but he would just correct me. Thank you for pushing me, Mike, and constantly making me smarter about all things location-based. And thank you for always having my back.

Mike Schneider: First and foremost is family: I would like to thank my wife, Jaye, for her love and support in everything that I do and for making our family the first priority. Thank you Mom, Dad, Dan, and Matt (and to my grandparents, aunts, uncles, and cousins) for never correcting my stubborn desire to always find the next shiny thing and for always encouraging me to tell you what I thought about it.

Thank YOU for reading this book and for having the courage to pass it along to someone who needs it more than you. Tell them you are not calling them a Dummy; blame us.

I would like to thank Andrew Graff and the team at Allen & Gerritsen for endorsing this effort, for being a forward-thinking, quick, and nimble team, and for being the foundation that makes the things that I talk about possible. Thank you Aaron Strout for your friendship and for asking me to partner on this project. Thank you Melanie Strout for being his better half.

Thank you to my home city of Boston and especially organizations like the *Boston Globe, Boston Business Journal,* MITX, and The Ad Club for encouraging my behavior. Thank you Lisa Desisto, Lisa Van Der Pool, Kathy Kiley, Kate McCabe, Jaime Reynolds, Kiki Mills, Debi Kleiman, and Ellis Reavey. Thank you clients, especially those who have asked for our team's counsel on social, local, mobile, digital, and emerging technology efforts. Thank you for having the guts to innovate.

Thank you Gregory Ng for testing into this stuff with me and for always being way more than a sounding board. Thank you Alex Meyer for being Alex Meyer. Thanks Jiffanimal. Thanks Kevin Long for always checking in on everything.

Thank you to the innovators in the space, particularly Josh Williams, Dennis Crowley, Naveen Selvardurai, Jeff Holden, Seth Priebatsch, Andy Ellwood, BJ Emerson, Casey Petersen, Walt Doyle, Ryan Kuder, Nataly Kogan, Gadi Shamia, Jyri Engstrom, DJ Patil, John Kim, Matt Galligan, Mok Oh, David Chang, Dan Gilmartin, AT Fouty, Lenny Rachitsky, and Rob Lawson. Thank you Gary Vaynerchuk for constant inspiration. Thank you to all of the event organizers, promoters, and their teams who have given me a platform and for allowing me to plug the book, the agency, and whatever else I've been working on: Jason Keath and Social Fresh, Rick Calvert, Deb Ng, and the entire BlogWorld team, Bonin Bough, Josh Karpf, Xiaochang Li and the PepsiCo team for the sponsorship and stage at SXSW, Hugh and the gang at SXSW, Chris Barger, Mark Evans from Social Loco, Chris Valentine, Laurel Ruma, Brady Forrest, Tonia Ries, Anne Weiskopf, the WOMMA gang, Tyson Goodridge and The Eat Drink and Be Social team, Heather Meeker, Chris Brogan and Inbound Marketing Summit, Chris Pirillo, Geekazine, and everyone else past and future. Thank you Chris Thompson for your tireless work with AboutFoursquare.com. Special thanks to the Future of Local: Phil Thomas DiGiulio and Pamela Granoff. Thank you to Austin and Seattle who with Boston form the Triangle of Awesome. Thanks you Ginger Man American Craft, and The Half Pint.

Anyone who ever said that writing a For Dummies book was easy — was wrong! No dummy is a dummy; people who read these books know that everyone needs to start somewhere. Thank you to Wiley, especially our editing team Amy Fandrei, Rebecca Senninger, and Heidi Unger for keeping us honest, helping us establish our voices and pace, and for your patience. Thank you Rebecca Sullivan for being one of my biggest supporters. Thank you Russian River Brewing Company in beautiful Santa Rosa, CA, for Pliny the Elder — a product that constantly inspires me to be the very best. Last but not least, HUGE thanks to Eric Leist and Elizabeth Sklar for your contributions and for making coming to work every day awesome.

Now, get out there and manufacture some serendipity!

Publisher's Acknowledgments

We're proud of this book; please send us your comments at http://dummies.custhelp.com. For other comments, please contact our Customer Care Department within the U.S. at 877-762-2974, outside the U.S. at 317-572-3993, or fax 317-572-4002.

Some of the people who helped bring this book to market include the following:

Acquisitions and Editorial

Project Editor: Rebecca Senninger

Acquisitions Editor: Amy Fandrei

Copy Editor: Heidi Unger

Technical Editors: Chris Banks and Asif Khan

Editorial Manager: Leah Cameron

Editorial Assistant: Amanda Graham

Sr. Editorial Assistant: Cherie Case

Cover Photo: ©istockphoto.com / Maksym Yemelynov

Cartoons: Rich Tennant (www.the5thwave.com)

Composition Services

Project Coordinator: Patrick Redmond

Layout and Graphics: Lavonne Roberts, Corrie Socolovitch

Proofreader: Melissa Cossell, Kimberly Holtman

Indexer: Glassman Indexing Services

Publishing and Editorial for Technology Dummies

   Richard Swadley, Vice President and Executive Group Publisher

   Andy Cummings, Vice President and Publisher

   Mary Bednarek, Executive Acquisitions Director

   Mary C. Corder, Editorial Director

Publishing for Consumer Dummies

   Kathy Nebenhaus, Vice President and Executive Publisher

Composition Services

   Debbie Stailey, Director of Composition Services

Contents at a Glance

Table of Contents

Foreword

. . . .

You have in your hands a brilliant resource written by two of the best thought leaders and strategists in the industry. As an early navigator in this space, I've watched Mike and Aaron help lead the way, and I'm honored to be able to provide an introduction to what I hope will help propel you into the bright and promising future of location-based marketing.

I'm sure by now you've observed customers using mobile apps to not only locate and review, but interact with local businesses. Perhaps a client has inquired about them, you've seen a competitor advertise their use of one of these platforms, or you just want to reach customers where they are. Either way, you can see the potential for these applications in your business and don't want to miss out on the next wave of new social technologies.

Location-based services have allowed the "where" dimension to come of age and have taken the opportunities for customer acquisition and engagement to a whole new level. This new context of location has marketers everywhere scrambling for a foothold as consumers migrate in droves to smartphones, mobile devices, and applications that allow them to share their whereabouts with friends and followers. Many times these activities revolve around brand venues and local businesses, and these virtual endorsements are allowing customers to share their affinity for a product or business in real time within a community of their closest and most trusted friends.

Good news: there's a new metric in town. For years we have been limited to mere impressions and clicks. Enter the check-in, the confirmation of an actual foot-in-the-door visit to a physical location. The addition of this key piece of information unlocks a new world of opportunities. As well, if you've ever been challenged by the chasm that exists between the online customer engagement and the in-store experience, this is your chance to help bridge the gap.

Reaching consumers based on their current proximity to your business is no longer a futuristic concept. It is a present reality, and many are already reaping great benefits. For merchants big and small, location-based services have leveled the playing field when it comes to raising awareness and attracting and retaining customers as well as rewarding them for their loyalty.

You'll see in this book references to the Old West. Things are still a little wild in LBS, and there is much unexplored territory, with opportunities to pioneer new applications, solutions, and integrations. With this book, you have equipped yourself to do just that and be a part of one of the most significant movements in the history of marketing and technology. The possibilities are endless, and your potential is limited only by your ability to design and implement creative campaigns.

BJ Emerson
VP Technology, Tasti D-Lite

Introduction

For smart marketers and business owners, the goal has always been to know as much about your customers as possible. Unfortunately, one of the most relevant pieces of data about a customer is where the customer is at any given time during the day, which leaves marketing professionals wishing for information that they most often 'don't have access to. With the advent of location-based services (LBS), this wish is granted, thanks to platforms like foursquare, Facebook Places, and SCVNGR.

With one in every four adults in the U.S. owning a smartphone and the number of mobile users who reported "checking in" with a location-based service in the United States approaching 10 percent, the possibility of reaching a meaningful swath of consumers with location-based services — and more importantly, knowing where they are during the day — is becoming a reality. While it may still take another 12–18 months for location-based activity to hit critical mass, now is the time for you to tap into this exciting new marketing opportunity.

About This Book

Location-Based Marketing For Dummies is the first book to provide a pragmatic yet thorough approach for marketers, social media practitioners, and small business owners to tapping into the power of location-based services. Because this is still a relatively new field, very few blogs, books, and other resources help spell out the roadmap for a successful location-based campaign. And like other *For Dummies* books, this book offers a blueprint for which services to consider, how to claim a location, thinking through an offer, and then testing, measuring, and optimizing an LBS campaign. *Location-Based Marketing For Dummies* is full of tips, suggestions, and visuals to help anyone from the novice to the adept marketer understand the ins and outs of using LBSs.

Foolish Assumptions

We make a few assumptions about you as the marketing professional or small business owner in this book:

✔ You don't use an abacus to do complex math.

✔ You have a smartphone or tablet like the iPhone, Droid, or Samsung Galaxy.

✔ You're familiar with basic computer concepts and terminology.

✔ You have permission to run a location-based campaign for your company as either the owner, an employee, or an authorized agency partner.

How This Book Is Organized

We organized this book into five parts. Each part is comprised of two to four chapters. Each chapter offers recommendations on how to use location-based services to engage with your customers.

Part 1: Putting a Little "Location" in Your Marketing Campaign

If you want to get started with your own location-based marketing campaign and understanding the basics like who the players are, which services they provide, how to chose the right services for your business along with the nuts and bolts of the game mechanics behind these services, Part I is a great place to start. In particular, we offer a matrix of the top players by type, what their unique value proposition is, and what business goal they might help you solve.

Part II: Location-Based Marketing in Action

In Part II of the book, we get into the nuts and bolts of building a campaign. We show you how to build, test, and optimize a campaign using location-based services. In this part, we also dig deep into the elements of a good offer as well as tell you how you can leverage your location-based services of choice to create a loyalty program.

Part III: Integrating Location into Other Channels

For anyone interested in the 201- or 301-level courses of location-based marketing, Part III dives deeper into how to integrate your campaign into other social networks like Twitter and Facebook. Chapter 9 also dives into ways to think about location beyond just LBSs, including Google, Yelp, and Bing.

Part IV: Measuring Your Return on Investment

For all you measurement and analytics types, Part IV is a must-read. In this part, we drill down on key performance indicators, dashboards, and measurement techniques for location-based marketing campaigns. Even if your eyes glaze over at the thought of spreadsheets and anything measurement-related, don't skip this section — you'd be doing your campaign a big disservice.

Part V: The Part of Tens

For us, Part V, The Part of Tens, was the most fun part of the book to write. These are chapters that cover ancillary topics like 10 reasons why you would want to use a location-based service provider versus building an LBS yourself and another twenty LBS companies to keep an eye on over the coming months. The last chapter talks about ten additional ways to market your location-based campaign offline.

Appendixes

We also include two appendixes, which are purely optional but provide a little more detail about the technology that enables location-based services and a primer on how to participate in these services as an end user. The first appendix speaks to your inner geek and may help you sound smart(er) if one of your customers asks you a question about how/why this stuff works. The second appendix will get you up to speed if you haven't used location-based services before and help you better understand the experience from your customers' vantage point.

You'll also find a cheat sheet with additional content at `www.dummies.com/cheatsheet/locationbasedmarketing`.

Icons Used in This Book

 We use the following icons to highlight particular parts of the text:

This icon points out useful, but not essential, information regarding a particular topic.

 This icon highlights information that's important and might even be worth writing down.

 This icon — while used infrequently — notes things not to do when running a location-based marketing campaign.

 This icon points to tips that only techies and IT-minded folks may want to use. If you just want the basics, you can feel free to ignore the technical stuff.

Where to Go from Here

You can start at Chapter 1 and keep reading until you get to the end or you can look up a topic that interests you in the table of contents or index and flip to the page you need and then put the book down until you need it again. Either way works for us.

If you've already launched a campaign or are well-steeped in how the technology works, you can skip some of the introductory chapters. In particular:

- If you already use location-based services and have claimed a venue, you can skip to Part II.

- If you want to focus on measurement and optimization, go to Part IV.

- If you're ready to create a great offer, Chapter 6 is where you'll want to check in.

- If you like doing things backward and you're more interested in understanding how to use location-based services from a personal perspective, hop right to Appendix B. It's a primer on using LBS.

- If you have a pretty good sense of how location-based marketing works but want to know how to turn it into more of a loyalty play, you can fast-forward to Chapter 7.

Contact Us!

We want to hear from you. You can find us at the following places:

- ✔ **A blog devoted to location-based marketing:** `http://location-basedmarketingfordummies.com`. We'll provide updates for where we're speaking, online and offline. We'll also cross-post the best of our location blog posts here.

- ✔ **On Twitter:** Send us tweets. `@aaronstrout` and `@schneidermike`

- ✔ **Our blogs:** Aaron's blog is `http://blog.stroutmeister.com/`. Mike's is `http://schneidermike.com`.

Good luck with your location-based marketing program!

Part I

Putting a Little "Location" in Your Marketing Campaign

The 5th Wave   By Rich Tennant

©RICHTENNANT

"Sometimes I feel behind the times. I asked my 11-year old to build a foursquare page for my business, and he said he would, only after he finished the one he's building for his ant farm."

In this part . . .

So you want to know about location-based marketing? Buying this book is a step in the right direction. Now it's time to roll up your sleeves and dig into the who, where, and why of location-based marketing. In this part, we cover these topics:

- ✔ The background of location-based services (LBS) and some of the privacy concerns that need to be considered

- ✔ Which location-based services you should consider and why

- ✔ The game mechanics and why people choose to check in

Chapter 1

Understanding Location-Based Services

In This Chapter

▶ Understanding what makes people check in

▶ Tapping into other social networks to spread the word

▶ Understanding the components of location-based networks

▶ The importance of privacy when using LBS

*I*f you're reading this book, there is at least a 50 percent chance that you've heard of a company called foursquare. If not, we're almost certain you've heard of a service called Yelp. No? Well, we know that you absolutely, positively have heard of a little company in Silicon Valley called Facebook. You have? Okay, good. You've come to the right place.

What do these three companies have in common? They all provide some form of a *location-based service* (LBS), a service that uses the geographical position of a mobile device. These services can be fun or for serious business (or both). In this book, we focus on the business side — how to use these location-based services for marketing your business.

According to comScore, 7.1 percent of all online U.S. adults accessed check-in services like Facebook Places and foursquare in March of 2011. This number has grown to 7.1 percent over the past year for a couple of major reasons: Facebook's leap into the LBS space with Places and an increased commitment by businesses to step up offers and value add. Something worth noting (as shown in Figure 1-1) is that over the last 18 months, the base of location-based services users has begun to skew slightly to female.

According to a number of sources, over the next couple of years, the adoption of smartphones is anticipated to grow more than 50 percent, resulting in dramatic increases of location-based services usage. As a result of the rich data, engagement, and loyalty that LBSs facilitate, more and more businesses are adopting these technologies.

The genesis of the location-based service

Some of the earlier LBS pioneering can be attributed to programs like the infrared Active Badge system (1989–1993), Microsoft's Wi-Fi–based indoor location system RADAR (2000), the MIT' Cricket project using ultrasound location (2000), and the Intel' Place Lab with wide-area location (2003). However, the first LBS to gain any kind of critical mass was Dodgeball (now foursquare), founded by NYU students Dennis Crowley and Alex Rainert in 2000 and then later acquired by Google in 2005. Dodgeball was later spun off by Google and ultimately reincorporated as the current foursquare. Loopt was the next big LBS to come on the scene in 2005, followed by Brightkite in 2007.

Figure 1-1: comScore's demographics of U.S adult mobile users who accessed check-in services in March, 2011.

Demographic Profile of US Smartphone vs. Total Mobile Phone Users Who Are Check-In Service* Users, March 2011 % of respondents			
	% of total mobile users	% of smartphone users	% of check-in service users
Gender			
Male	48.0%	53.9%	49.2%
Female	52.0%	46.1%	50.8%
Age			
13-17	7.1%	6.0%	8.3%
18-24	12.5%	17.5%	26.0%
25-34	17.6%	27.3%	32.5%
35-44	16.8%	21.8%	18.7%
45-54	17.8%	15.0%	9.7%
55-64	14.1%	7.8%	3.0%
65+	14.0%	4.7%	1.7%
Employment			
Full time	38.9%	53.3%	46.6%
Part time	10.5%	9.0%	10.2%
Not employed but not retired	15.1%	12.5%	13.5%
Full-time student	14.6%	16.5%	23.3%
Retired or other	20.9%	8.8%	6.3%

Note: numbers may not add up to 100% due to rounding; three-month average for period ending March 2011; *e.g., Facebook Places, foursquare and Gowalla
Source: comScore MobiLens as cited in press release, May 12, 2011
127842   www.eMarketer.com

Courtesy of eMarketer, Inc.

Defining a Check-in: The Ultimate Goal

Check-ins are at the center of location-based marketing. You get someone to check in to your location and give them a reason to spend money with you.

Similar to checking in to a hotel or flight, a *check-in* is a declaration that "I am here." Check-ins are interesting because they also give you a way track who is at your location at a given point in time.

There are two kinds of check-ins:

- **Active:** A person physically pushes a button on his phone or device to check in.
- **Passive:** A person's device or an action (such as swiping a loyalty card) checks him in without him having to do anything.

With the active check-in, which is more common in location-based services, you're asking your customers to use their valuable time to perform a small task, which we outline next. And then we tell you about the types of information you might collect from these check-ins.

Additional check-in definitions

We asked members of the senior teams of several leading location-based providers to define the term. Here are some check-in definitions from leaders in the space:

A check-in is a digital record that a person visited a specific named place in the real world at a specific time. It has a couple of very interesting properties. First, it's far more valuable than just location because it gives the context of "place'" — is the person at the Outback Restaurant or the pharmacy next door? And place is subject to analysis: "people who go to place X also go to place Y," or "this person frequents this place or these kinds of places." From a business perspective, place enables the development of programs (loyalty/rewards, games) tied to specific businesses. Another key property is that check-ins happen in real time — they communicate "I'm here right now." That opens opportunities for social connection in the moment.

> Jeff Holden, CEO Pelago, Makers of Whrrl (now part of Groupon)

A check-in, broadly speaking, is a way to share your location — and more broadly what you're doing at that location — with your friends. In many ways, a check-in is a standardized greeting in a conversation about what's going on at a place. It provides a structured framework for the conversation, but the interesting part is the content that comes after the 'hello.'

> Seth Priebatsch, Chief Ninja, SCVNGR

We think of a check-in as a way for users to opt-in and share their locations with friends or other applications and services. At foursquare, we also use check-in data to help surface interesting content, such as nearby friends' recommendations for things to do or places to visit, and special offers from retailers. We see the check-in as the atomic unit in creating technology that facilitates serendipity.

> Dennis Crowley, cofounder and CEO of foursquare

Checking in is the match that lights the fire. It's the social declaration of "I'm here!" that opens the door to seeing the world around you through a new set of eyes: Who is here? What can I do nearby? What secrets are there to learn here? It's not the end. It's only the beginning.

> Josh Williams, CEO of Gowalla

Check-in is a way to indicate your location at a particular place, and, if the check-in is public, share it with your friends. In its simplest form, it's a status update, indicating where someone is at a particular time.

> Nataly Kogan, Vice President, Director of Consumer Experience for WHERE

Understanding check-in behavior

To be successful with location-based marketing, you have to understand what you're asking customers to do when they check in. Here are the general steps participants go through to check in to your location:

1. Take out a phone when they enter your location.

2. Open an application from a location-based service.

3. Search through a list of places that are nearby the current location as defined by the phone's GPS.

4. Select a place (or search if the place they're at is not on the list).

5. Touch a Check-in button.

6. (Optional) Share the fact that they just checked in with other social networks.

7. (Optional) See what happens after they check in — maybe a friend is in the same location.

8. (Optional) Add tips, recommendations, photos, or additional content to the check-in.

Not a lot of people are going to want to do this much work or look as if they're doing something strange. You have to be able to overcome that obstacle by making your location-based campaigns easy to use. People are willing to do almost anything if they see the value in it and it's easy to do.

Make your check-ins as passive as possible. Technology exists that allows someone to check in to a service by merely walking into your store or scanning a barcode with a phone.

The anatomy of a check-in

So what does a check-in look like? Figure 1-2 shows what a typical check-in looks like on foursquare, one of the richest and most-used location-based services.

Each service is a bit different in what it provides and the features it offers. But in general, here's what you find in a check-in:

✔ **The person who currently has the most check-ins:** See who the person is that checks in to the location you're checking in to most frequently. That person probably knows a few tips and tricks about the business. (foursquare calls this person the mayor, as shown in Figure 1-2.)

✔ **Friends:** If any of your friends are checked in to the venue, their pictures will appear under the mayor.

✔ **Location:** The address appears under the venue name. At the bottom of the screen (not visible), click a link for additional information to see phone numbers, Twitter handles, and directions.

✔ **Tips:** If other users (or you) have added tips or comments about the venue, click a link to access all of them.

✔ **Photos:** Similar to tips, you can also see whether any photos have been uploaded to the venue you checked in to.

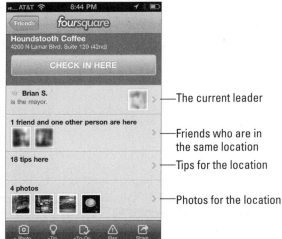

Figure 1-2:
A
foursquare
check-in.

The current leader

Friends who are in the same location

Tips for the location

Photos for the location

Understanding the Key Factors of LBS

When you start with location-based marketing, it's critical to understand two of the underlying forces driving its evolution and development. In particular, mobile technology and social networking play a critical role in shaping what's possible for location-based marketing.

Mobile technology

Mobile technology has played a tremendous role in the adoption of LBS. In particular, the FCC mandate that GPS technology has to be included with cell-phones unlocked the ability for geo-awareness. GPS combined with the mass adoption of *smartphones* (phones that have functionality beyond just making phone calls and sending text messages) is driving increased adoption of LBS, particularly among influential, affluent males.

Until a few years ago, there were primarily six different mobile operating systems:

- **Symbian:** Standard operating system for a large majority of the world's smartphones (including Nokia).

- **BlackBerry:** The device and operating system of choice for most large enterprises, the BlackBerry OS from Research in Motion was one of the most popular operating system in the United States until a few years ago.

- **Windows Mobile:** Available on a variety of devices from a variety of wireless operators.

- **Palm OS:** Launched in 1996, the Palm OS platform has provided mobile devices with essential business tools as well as the capability to access the Internet.

- **Mobile Linux:** Linux is seen as a suitable option for higher-end phones with powerful processors and larger amounts of memory.

- **MXI:** A universal mobile operating system that allows existing full-fledged desktop and mobile applications written for Windows, Linux, Java, and Palm enabled immediately on mobile devices without any redevelopment.

Now add to this list the likes of iOS (Apple devices like iPhone and iPad), Android, Nokia's Ovi, and Palm's newer webOS, and you have a lot of different platforms to support. Fortunately, three of the operating systems — iOS, Android, and Symbian — make up the lion's share of the market. In your case, it's probably easier to think about types of devices and not worry as much about platform because there are three major categories of devices on the market today:

- **Smartphones:** These mainly comprise phones made by Nokia (including the C7 and 6303Xx), Apple (iPhone), HTC (Thunderbolt), Motorola (Droid), and Research In Motion (BlackBerry).

- **Tablets:** At this point, there are really too many to list, but Apple created this market with its iPad. Dell, HP, and a number of other PC manufacturers have created offerings in this category as well.

- **Laptops, notebooks, and netbooks:** This is a relatively new category and is pushing out an earlier category known as personal digital assistants (PDAs). Palm owned this market early on but ultimately lost this footrace to the likes of today's smartphone giants Nokia, Apple, Samsung, RIM, and HTC.

To illustrate the point of how the user interface for a venue on a single LBS can change across different devices, Figure 1-3 shows how the same venue on the same LBS (Yelp) looks on three different devices. At the top of Figure 1-3 is the web version of a local Starbucks's Yelp entry. The bottom-left image in Figure 1-3 shows the same venue in Yelp on an iPad, which shows a much different view. The bottom right of Figure 1-3 shows an even more scaled-down view of the entry, as it appears on an iPhone.

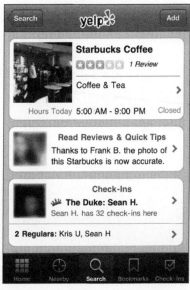

Figure 1-3: An LBS page on a MacBook Pro, iPad, and iPhone, respectively.

All your customers will experience your venue differently across their various mobile devices. This does not mean that you have to go out and buy one of every device on the market, but it doesn't hurt to at least have an idea of what your venue(s) look like on PC versus Mac versus smartphone versus tablet.

One last point: If you have a tech-savvy customer base that's spread across numerous mobile platforms and devices, this may play a role in your LBS platform decision.

Digital platforms and media

One of the things that will only become more prevalent over the next couple of years is *geotargeting* (or serving up messages and offers based on location) as a part of advertising. For example, adding location to services such as DART for Publishers (an online ad-serving system now owned by Google). One thing that you can start thinking about as you test location-based services is how you could use your LBS or recommendation engines like WHERE (or even Twitter) to start to serve more relevant ads to your customers.

What's really exciting about the promise of geotargeted advertising is that this comes with the advantage of *day-parting* (serving up time-sensitive ads, such as lunch ads around noon) and demographic targeting. Most important is that your customers, or prospective customers, will actually have a way to act on these targeted ads via an LBS.

Social networking

Another part of the equation that will continue to drive the adoption of LBS is the increased popularity of social networks such as Facebook and Twitter. With Facebook accounting for one out of every four page views on the web in the United States, people are spending a lot of time networking. Part of what makes social experiences richer with friends and family is not just knowing "what" they're doing but "where" they're doing it. Location-based services go a long way toward facilitating the "where."

From a personal perspective, many people using location-based services today do so because of the gaming factor — earning badges and winning prizes. Others do so to gain social credibility by letting their friends know that they're at a concert, cool bar, or trendy restaurant.

Looking at the power of social networking from a business perspective, they're equally if not more so motivated to have their customers not only checking in to their physical locations, but also sharing these check-ins with their social networks.

The force that drives social networking is the social graph. A *social graph* consists of everyone that someone is connected to online: friends, family, former classmates, co-workers, and neighbors. Services like Facebook and Twitter keep this collection of connections centralized and accessible by other applications. When a user creates a social graph, other applications such as Gowalla or Yelp can grab that social graph, and that information can be easily shared across more networks.

Physical locations

The four walls and the space within them will start to become more important in the world of location-based marketing. Right now, a majority of LBS providers rely on GPS to allow customers to check in to a venue. Only shopkick — a company that powers LBS programs for the likes of Simon Malls, Sports Authority, Target, and Best Buy, among many others — requires retail stores to install physical hardware in their store that will passively check in customers if they have the shopkick application open on their smartphone.

In addition to passive check-ins relying on physical in-store hardware, you will also start to see more LBS and businesses using *geofencing,* which is isolating a particular location for privacy reasons. But as more companies adopt LBS and offer richer offers to incentivize customers to check in, concerns around "gaming the system" will grow. To combat this problem, geofencing allows tighter controls over ensuring that a customer is physically in your venue (or at least within a 20-yard perimeter).

As Wi-Fi, 3G and 4G, LTE, WiMax microwaves, and other forms of delivering connectivity to mobile devices become more pervasive with an ability to cover longer distances, this will create a need for LBS to create enough elasticity around its check-in rules. For example, someone can go from a Wi-Fi network (which can sometimes interfere with GPS) to a 3G or 4G network, and then pick up public Wi-Fi networks. Location-based providers have to understand these patterns and not penalize customers if a local coffee shop's Wi-Fi connects to a router five miles away and thus makes it appear that the customer is not actually in the store but rather next to the building housing the router.

There is a fairly straightforward fix for a router that isn't correctly broadcasting your store's location. A service called Skyhook keeps a database of Wi-Fi spots and their locations. Many LBSs use Skyhook's data to determine a Wi-Fi user's location, so if your location is incorrect in that database, LBS users might have trouble checking in at your venue. You can update your location in the Skyhook database by following the steps at `http://www.stationripper.com/iphone_foursquare_correcting_location.htm`.

Digging into the Differences between Place and Location

As a marketer or business owner, you'll find that as you get into using location-based services as part of your marketing mix, you will start to understand the nuances between what makes something a location versus a place. In fact, understanding the difference between the two (think of the semantical differences between a *house* and a *home*) is key to creating a great LBS experience for your customers.

Location is a fixed coordinate, a point on the planet, and although its attributes may change over time, the location never does. An easier way to look at a location is to translate it into longitude and latitude — the way any location in the world is precisely mapped by map makers and government agencies. To that end, location by itself is not interesting for marketing purposes.

When you take a location and make it into place, then you can start marketing. The attributes help answer questions and tell you how to craft your message.

If you take a location like that of the Russian River Brewery and present it in terms of longitude and latitude — 38.441775, -122.71162 — it means very little unless you are a cartographer. However, try adding some additional metadata like that provided on the business's foursquare page shown in Figure 1-4, and you have a location.

Figure 1-4:
Russian
River
Brewery's
foursquare
page exhib-
its many
of the key
traits of a
place.

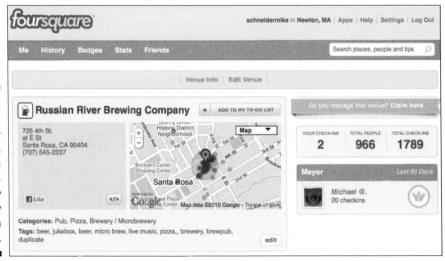

Adding points of interest to location and place

Here is why the distinction between location, place, and point of interest are important. It is easy to understand location. It is a set of latitudes and longitudes on a map. Place brings context to a location. It allows you to have a conversation about the place Austin in the larger place Texas instead of having a conversation about all of the points of latitude and longitude on the map that define the borders of Texas and then the points that define the borders of Austin. Places are agreed upon and defined, and they give you a way to talk about a location. Points of interest are defined but are not necessarily agreed upon. For example, you could find a gorgeous flower patch in a location. You might mark it with a pin on the map. This now becomes a point of interest for you, but it may not be agreed upon by the community at large. Still, you gave it context, and that matters for anyone who understands your context.

A *place,* in terms of location-based marketing, has attributes like these:

✔ Series of coordinates, locations

✔ Name

✔ Street name and address

✔ Cross-street

✔ City

✔ State

✔ Category

✔ Multiple tags to describe the place

✔ A check-in leader

✔ Check-ins

Dealing with Privacy Concerns

One of the biggest obstacles preventing location-based services from really catching fire is privacy. Consumers are rightly anxious when it comes to broadcasting where they are, in any particular moment. You need to be clear in your answers to the following questions:

✔ When participants check in, who exactly is seeing their whereabouts?

✔ How do you target groups of people?

✔ Are participants putting others at risk if people know their exact whereabouts?

Sharing a location, as with sharing anything online, can cause problems. Customers need to be comfortable with people seeing their data. You're asking them to become in essence public figures. Make it clear in your terms and agreements what customers will be divulging in terms of what data is shared and in what application.

Here are a couple ways you can encourage people to check in a little more privately:

- ✔ **Off-grid check-ins:** The platforms are making attempts to address privacy. Some allow customers to check in and share information with the platform, but not with the public. In foursquare, this is called an *off-grid* check-in.

  A check-in may not stay off the grid. If a friend mentions someone in his check-in, the previous off-grid check-in is suddenly public.

- ✔ **Private groups:** Whrrl (now part of Groupon) used a model that allowed someone to name two groups of people who can see check-ins: friends and trusted friends. It gave users another level of privacy. Although Whrrl no longer exists in its current state, other LBSs may provide this type of functionality in the future.

- ✔ **Geofencing:** Geofencing is a passive check-in where someone merely walks into a predetermined area. A *geofence* is a series of locations that forms an area. Users can set them up to make sure that onlookers cannot see their whereabouts when they are inside the geofence.

- ✔ **Microsharing:** Applications like Glympse allow customers to give an exact location to a series of people for a specified period of time.

Treating others as you wish to be treated is a good start, but here are a few other things to remember:

- ✔ **Be transparent.**

  Make sure users know exactly what you want to collect from them and how it will be used.

- ✔ **Keep your requests simple.**

  Do not ask for too much from your users. Make the requests easy to understand and don't try to do too many things. If you confuse them, they will be leery of trusting your campaign. Make sure they see the link to the data you are requesting and the reward they are receiving. The reward should be commensurate with the amount of data they are providing.

- ✔ **Protect their identity.**

  Do not sell participants' data or expose their identities without their permission. See rule #1.

Chapter 2

Surveying the Location-Based Services Landscape

*I*n this chapter, we explore the world of location-based services (LBSs). Like many sectors with large amounts of potential, there are multiple ideas about how to define the boundaries of the space, and often there are disagreements to how the space should ultimately be defined.

Location-based services all have one thing in common: They create semantic information around the concept of a place. *Semantic information* means that the way the data is expressed is via a set of common attributes. A place contains a name, address, description, category, and phone number. Some of that data — such as the category — is even standardized, which means that you have only a finite number of values to choose from.

Categorizing Services

The first thing to do when navigating the myriad of services is to group them into these categories:

✔ **Mobile:** Mobile location-based services give you the ability to reach just about anybody with a mobile phone in the place that they are at the time that they need the information. You may assume that all location-based services are mobile because of the strong association of location and global positioning systems and the fact that all mobile phones have GPS. Companies build applications to run on smartphones— such as Apple's iPhone, the HTC Incredible that runs Google's popular Android operating system, and many others.

Mobile applications can also be accessed via the (mobile) web. While many companies favor building applications that are delivered via stores like iTunes, Android Market, Blackberry's App World, and many more, developers can also deliver applications via the mobile web and SMS (text messaging) so that feature phones (mobile phones that don't have the same computing power that smartphones have) can also get some of the benefits, if not the richness of the experience. This opens location-based services to every mobile handset user, as long as the company is willing to maintain several versions of applications for various kinds of handsets.

✔ **Check-in:** One of the most common application types is the check-in. A *check-in* is the ability to announce "I am here." The idea is simple, but the barriers to entry are high, though, as checking in to a location isn't very useful on its own. The check-in can deliver a lot of highly standard data for you to analyze: the person, place, and time.

Knowing that a person checked in to a place allows you to begin to build profiles of users who check in to your business. Those profiles can tell a story about who checks in and why they check in.

✔ **Social:** What good is a check-in if nobody knows? Social applications allow users to maintain a list of trusted friends that they can share the information with. Location-based applications allow users to share check-ins with a wide range of entities, including friends, colleagues, business associates, and even strangers. Some services allow a user to share this information through other social applications, too. In other words, a location-based application — such as foursquare — might plug into a larger network like Twitter or Facebook. As a marketer, you want to encourage your customers to tap into these networks to spread the word about your business.

✔ **Discovery:** When you talk about location, you have to talk about discovery, or *manufactured serendipity*. Serendipity is accidental discovery, which is one of the driving forces behind the popularity of LBSs. Location-based services can document the secrets of your business through content attached to places in the form of pictures, recommendations, and even video.

Making recommendations — helping others discover businesses, places, products, and services that they might enjoy — isn't limited to the application users. You can add tips in places to help customers unlock the secrets of your business. Some platforms offer users the ability to declare that they saw your tip and tried your recommendation. The associated metrics become another way to demonstrate the effectiveness of the campaign.

Applications in this category include Bizzy, WHERE, Yelp, foursquare, Gowalla, Ditto, and Foodspotting.

✔ **Engagement:** Some location-based services allow you to have a conversation. Engagement is a one-to-one, more personal sort of conversation than just blasting "here I am" to a bunch of people. If you can carry on a dialogue or group conversation, this is engagement. Think of Twitter and Facebook as the ultimate platforms for engagement and having some (not all) of their abilities to communicate one to one within the location-based service.

✔ **Ambient:** Ambient networks use the device's environment to do interesting things like building a social graph without the input of the user. These networks use attributes like place, time, and even the noise in the room to see who is together and then decide who the user's friends are. To use this technology, encourage loyal customers to take pictures that represent your brand. Those customers are then lumped into the social graph of early adopters, and they can then interact with other early adopters and encourage others to join the fun. The full extent of opportunities with ambient networks is still unknown, but the possibilities are exciting.

Color is an ambient social network. Other ambient networks allow users to interact with each other based on proximity. They use chat rooms and text messaging to form temporary networks of people in a particular place. Brands can get involved in the conversation too but these technologies are just getting off the ground.

✔ **Future and Intent:** Sometimes you know what you're going to do and you want to let people know. Whether it's going to an event or having a coffee, you might want to let people know so that you can connect with them or solicit their opinions about what you should do. People like recommendations and advice from people they trust. They also like to know who's going to be at an event so that they can decide not only how they'll spend their time, but with whom. These LBS applications allow that to happen — and enable you to catch a customer right at their decision point and make a very relevant offer.

✔ **Platform:** Platforms allow you to take a set of functionality and build something else. Location-based platforms provide places databases, check-in functionality, tips and recommendations, authentication, and much more. You can use these platforms to build your own application to cater to your specific purposes.

✔ **Content network:** Some location-based systems have copious amounts of user-generated and publisher/professional content. User-generated content is created voluntarily by someone who isn't paid. Reviews on Amazon and Yelp, videos on YouTube, tweets on Twitter, plurks on Plurk, and highlights on Gowalla are all examples of user-generated content (UGC). Some of these platforms allow you to tailor your content that can be placed right next to the UGC.

✔ **Analysis:** A series of tools allow you to build campaigns and measure their impact. Some of them are location-specific and provide a look at what's happening in check-in spaces. Others require you to have the data, but provide strong tools for visualizing the impact.

Some of these analytic tools even allow you to execute campaigns while capturing best practices and campaign effectiveness.

✔ **Offers:** Many platforms let you offer specials and deals to people who check in at your place. The idea is that location adds contextual relevance. Sending the ideal offer exactly when someone needs it is the idea that marketers really latch onto.

Table 2-1 shows which location-based services fall into which category. This isn't an exhaustive list, but the table should give you a place to start exploring. In the next section, we talk more in depth about each of these services. Some we talk about throughout the book.

Table 2-1	**Services by Category**
Category	*Location-Based Services*
Mobile	Almost all (but most also have web versions like foursquare, Bizzy. Foodspotting, Gowalla)
Check-in	Almost all (for example, foursquare, Yelp, Gowalla)
Social	Almost all (any with an engagement model)
Discovery	Almost all (Gowalla, SCVNGR, WHERE, foursquare, and Bizzy stand out)
Future/Intent	Ditto Plancast Zaarly
Platform	foursquare FWIX SimpleGeo Factual Gowalla
Content Network	Bing for Business Google Places WHERE YP.com Yelp
Ambient/Proximity	Color LoKast Yobongo Locaii

Category	Location-Based Services
Analysis	Geotoko
	MomentFeed
	foursquare
Private	Geoloqi
	Glympse
	Neer
Offer	foursquare
	Google Latitude
	SCVNGR
	TriOut
	WHERE
	YP.com
	Yelp

Choosing Services

When it comes to selecting a location-based service, it can be hard finding the wheat through all the chaff. Throughout the book, we talk mostly about marketing via the heavy hitters: foursquare, Facebook Places, and Gowalla. In this section, we give you an overview of all the services that you'll find useful, divided into categories that might, in some way, fit your marketing needs.

You can choose more than one. Because most of these are free, you're risking only your time if one doesn't work for you.

The main players

The main players in the location-based space have a similar set of features. Each of them allows users to check in to a location, but each one has its own take on checking in. Some allow you to build offers, some promote retention and loyalty, and others focus on discovery.

  ✔ **Facebook Places:** Launched in August of 2010, Facebook Places (www.facebook.com/places) allows users to share where they are, connect with friends, and find local deals. Any of Facebook's 650 million users can use Facebook Places. You can reach the largest social networking audience with Facebook's Facebook Deals platform, but the customer service has been inferior to date, and getting analytics for campaigns is challenging.

Keep a very close eye on Facebook Places and its integration with the Facebook Deals platform, a daily-deals platform similar to Groupon.

- **foursquare:** The idea of the check-in first came to fruition with foursquare (www.foursquare.com). With over 10 million members (and growing at a faster rate than Twitter), foursquare is easily the most popular of all the LBS platforms. The system features check-ins, tips, badges, and points for accomplishments, a leaderboard, the most comprehensive specials platform, a way for users to explore nearby tips, and an application programming interface (API) that allows anyone to use its functionality to write their own applications.

- **Gowalla:** The Gowalla (www.gowalla.com) platform is dedicated to exploration and storytelling. Consider it a virtual passport. Users check in to places and collect stamps and virtual items along the way. Gowalla is focused on the user experience. Brands and users alike can create trips that help a user discover a series of places. Users are then given a pin to show that they completed the trip. Disney has been using these custom pins to help users explore the parks. USA Today created a series of trips to encourage exploration in major US cities.

- **SCVNGR:** Probably the most different from any of the other LBSs, SCVNGR (www.scvngr.com) lets you set up elaborate scavenger hunts. SCVNGR calls its platform a "game layer on top of the world." Aside from traditional scavenger hunts, it's ideal for creating a series of activities that act as a template to show users how to experience your brand. SCVNGR also has a rewards platform that allows you to give users incentives to do these tasks, which SCVNGR calls *challenges*.

- **WHERE:** WHERE (http://where.com) allows you to target consumers based on their location. In December 2010, WHERE was awarded a patent for *geofencing technology,* which allows events to be triggered when a user carrying a mobile phone enters a virtual area called a *geofence.* WHERE is one of the first LBSs to unlock the power of local advertising.

- **Yelp:** Founded in 2004, Yelp (www.yelp.com) was created with the intention of helping customers find great local businesses like dentists, hair stylists, and mechanics. As of January 2011, more than 45 million people visited Yelp in the past 30 days. Yelpers have written over 15 million local reviews. It also includes a specials platform. Aside from specials, Yelp allows you to advertise and add pictures of your place.

Photo-centric

By tying a picture to a place, users can add a layer of context to an LBS page and help tell the story of a place. Some services even use the smartphone's ability to capture the angle that the photo was taken, the noise in the location, and the place to decide if the people who took the photos were in the same place.

- ✔ **Instagram:** Leveraging foursquare's geolocation database, Instagram (http://instagr.am) provides a simple but elegant way to crop, apply filters, and then share images across multiple social networks including Facebook, Flickr, Twitter, Tumblr, Posterous, and foursquare. The drawback is that it's available for Apple iOS only. Chapter 15 includes more information on Instagram.

- ✔ **Color:** Using Color (www.color.com), you can connect with people who may have experienced a particular event together and help them experience different events after being automatically put into social networks.

- ✔ **Path:** Think of Path (www.path.com) as a way to share photos (tagged with geolocation data) and updates with a maximum number of connections. We go into more detail about Path in Chapter 15.

Path allows users to have only 50 connections. You can use it to share very exclusive content with a small group of your most loyal customers.

Discovery-oriented

Discovery-oriented LBSs are designed primarily with the idea of helping people find cool things in their area. These are built around user- and business-generated tips, and some of them are even smart enough to make recommendations based on the user's behavior and the behaviors of people that users trust.

- ✔ **Bizzy:** Looking for suggestions for a local barber, tanning salon, or steak-house? Bizzy (www.bizzy.com) provides recommendations based on a series of questions that users answer when signing up, combined with information about venues they've "checked out of."

To date, Bizzy is one of the few services that provide an ability to "check out" as opposed to "checking in." The idea of checking out is that you declare that you left as opposed to letting people know that you arrived. It also collects information about how you felt about the experience: in this case, there are three ratings. See Figure 2-1.

- ✔ **Loopt:** Even though Loopt (https://www.loopt.com) was one of the earlier players in the location-based space, they've struggled to stay relevant. Claiming over 3 million users, Loopt announced in late 2010 that they were scrapping their own geodatabase in favor of Facebook Places' database.

- ✔ **Loqly:** Loqly (http://loqly.me) answers users' questions using recommendations from people who are checked in to nearby restaurants and businesses.

Figure 2-1:
A user
checks out
on Bizzy
and lets the
application
know how
she felt
about the
experience.

Utilitarian

The utilitarian group of applications serves some interesting niche purposes. These apps allow people to find and locate other people. These types of apps are opportunities for you to get involved at low costs because these services aren't clearly defined. You could help craft, and test, marketing applications to these services.

- **Glympse:** Arguably one of the most useful location-based services of the bunch, this simple yet powerful app allows members to send other members and nonmembers their exact location via e-mail or text along with a short message. See Figure 2-2. This message contains a link that allows the recipient(s) to follow the sender for a preset period of time in real time, and it includes an estimated time of arrival. The recipient can follow the sender on a map and see here they are in real time via either the web or the Glympse app (www.glympse.com). Turn to Chapter 15 for more information on this service.

- **Google Latitude:** While Google is great at search, it has yet to crack the code on location-based services beyond one of the originals, Google Maps. Latitude (www.google.com/latitude) works similar to Facebook Places or foursquare in that members are allowed to check in. On the upside, this service leverages existing Google and Gmail profile data. On the downside, the uptake on this service and the gaming elements (badges, pins, and rewards) are minimal. You can also offer rewards via Google Latitude.

Figure 2-2:
Sending a
Glympse.

✔ **Neer:** Owned by mobile technology giant, Qualcomm, Neer (`www.neer life.com`) is similar to Glympse in the sense that it can share location with individuals versus wider groups of people. In addition, Neer also lets users set reminders that appear when the user has reached the designated area. For example, a user can set a reminder to buy paper towels at a specific store, and the reminder appears when the user's GPS detects that the user is at that store. Turn to Chapter 15 for more information on Neer.

✔ **Waze:** If you're familiar with General Motors' proprietary Turn-by-Turn Navigation service offered through OnStar, you'll immediately understand the value that Waze (`www.waze.com`) provides. This useful app provides turn-by-turn directions that are informed by traffic reports from other local users.

Food and beverage

People love to talk about food. This category highlights two popular applications in which you can feature foods and beverages in.

✔ **Foodspotting:** Also leveraging foursquare's geolocation database, Foodspotting (`www.foodspotting.com`) allows members to rate and review individual dishes at local restaurants. It also encourages users to upload photos of the dishes. Users can rate foods and places and share them with one another. Foodspotting gives the users a view of a location through the eyes of local foodies. Restaurants can have their dishes featured in guides that help people find specific types of food in a location. Brands like Zagat have built guides in Foodspotting. We cover Foodspotting in depth in Chapter 15.

✓ **Untappd:** This is the service that lets people check in to their beers. Similar to Foodspotting, Untappd (`www.untappd.com`) allows you to rate and review beer and let others know where you are while enjoying your beer and it's integrated with foursquare. Users can use the service to find out what kinds of beer are available at bars in their area. Some beer brands have used the badges feature to award users with a badge for checking in to their beers.

Deals

The deals space is full of options, including the three we highlight here.

✓ **Groupon:** Groupon (`www.groupon.com`) sends users an e-mail with a deal from 50–90 percent off of an item in their area. Users have 24 hours to opt in to the deal. If a predetermined number of people opt in to the deal in the 24-hour time frame, the deal is unlocked and everyone receives the deal.

Groupon acquired LBS mainstay Whrrl and built a new location-based service called Groupon Now. This allows you to build deals that are relevant for a certain period of time. Users can explore neighborhoods for deals using Groupon Now. They see the deal with a timer that shows how long the deal is relevant. They can buy the product from their phone or go to the business to redeem the offer. In the future, Whrrl features may be incorporated into Groupon Now.

✓ **shopkick:** shopkick (`www.shopkick.com`) allows brands to send people on a template experience. It beckons users to check into products in a store in exchange for kickbucks that they can redeem for free stuff. The idea of the application is that it gets users to explore a store, gives brands without brick-and-mortar locations a way to give people incentives to interact with their products, and gives the retailer a sense of where people are when they're in their store. shopkick also acts like a virtual circular, so to speak, alerting users to deals within the store when they check in. shopkick has deals in place with Best Buy, Target, Dick's Sporting Goods, and Simon Malls. See Figure 2-3.

✓ **CheckPoints:** Similar to shopkick, CheckPoints (`www.checkpoints.com`) is geared toward retailers and consumer packaged-goods companies. It provides points and virtual coins to users for signing up for new applications and scanning products in stores.

Figure 2-3:
A deal on
shopkick.

Planning

One of the interesting things about location and behavior is the idea of getting to a person at a decision point. These offerings are focused specifically on the notion of helping people express what they're going to do.

✔ **Ditto:** One of the few services that asks you where you plan to go versus where you actually are, Ditto (www.ditto.me) attempts to bridge the gaps among services like foursquare and Facebook Events. See Figure 2-4. It's a service that does these two very interesting things:

  • It allows users to semantically announce their desires. In other words, they choose what they want to do from a series of categories — such as home, food, coffee, movie, exercise, and more. These can then be further honed to subcategories — such as espresso, latte, French press, tea, or the specific film they want to see based on a list of current releases in the theater.

  • Wants are then tagged with a general vicinity the user is in.

You can monitor the service and provide users with information about products that fit their requests.

We talk more about Ditto in Chapter 15.

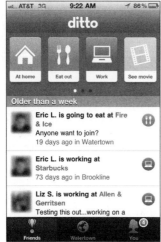

Figure 2-4:
Ditto starts
with a list
of popular
intentions.

✔ **Plancast:** Plancast (www.plancast.com) allows users to announce to friends and the public that they plan to attend an event. The entire service is built around events like concerts, conferences, tweetups, meetings, sporting events, and more. The service is integrated with Twitter and Facebook, so users can announce plans to the world.

Hopefully, Plancast will incorporate check-in services so that users can check-in to the event and venue simultaneously. Right now, it's fairly easy for a user to make a plan to go to an event, but not actually attend.

✔ **Zaarly:** Zaarly (www.zaarly.com) allows users to express very specific interests related to their location. Users tie a location to a need. They can say things like this: "I would like to stay in an apartment in Hell's Kitchen for two months, and I will pay $3,000;" "I would like a cheeseburger from Bill's Bar and Grill delivered to my hotel, and I will pay $50;" or "I would like to buy a new longboard, and I will spend up to $275." Businesses and people who can fulfill the need can create a minicontract on Zaarly and perform the service or provide the product.

Distribution services

These services allow you to push coupons and alerts to customers as they enter a predetermined area; you can snag new customers.

✔ **NAVTEQ:** A media solutions provider with a lot of available marketing services. Among NAVTEQ's (www.navteq.com) services is its LocationPoint advertising, focused on delivering the right messages to the right people at the right point in time. NAVTEQ also has a mapping and data visualization toolkit.

✔ **Placecast:** Carries the ability to deliver location-relevant coupons to your customers, as well as an ad distribution system that customizes mobile ads based on consumers' location. Placecast (`http://place cast.net`) also has a product for optimizing your venue page listings for mobile search.

✔ **AT&T ShopAlerts:** A subscription-based deals network available in only a few cities right now. Brands can partner with AT&T ShopAlerts (`http://shopalerts.att.com`) to send messages to AT&T's opt-in database. This service is actually powered by Placecast, but the value of AT&T's ShopAlerts is the aggregate partners who are in the network.

✔ **nSphere:** Provides localized advertising solutions, and with the recent purchase of Peekaboo mobile, nSphere (`www.directorym.com`) now has the ability to distribute location-based coupons through the native Peekaboo Mobile app as well as with other mobile application partners.

✔ **Valpak:** A coupon distribution network that has mobile and augmented reality capabilities. Valpak (`www.valpak.com`) focuses on targeting customers based on location, and offers a flexible pricing model.

Chapter 3

Choosing Platforms for Your Campaigns

....

....

*U*nless you're reading this book well into the future and the space has stabilized, you're probably currently hearing a lot about the value of location-based technology and are a little confused about how to choose which platform to focus on. In this chapter, we help you choose a platform.

At the time of publishing this book, we still liken the space to the Old West. Rules have not yet been clearly defined, terminology is disparate, business models are fluid, and (continuing the water analogy) because the market is flooded with options, you have a lot of choices when it comes to a location-based service.

There is a great opportunity to use technology for free, and this is the time to take advantage of that. Here, we cut through the confusing terminology and rules and help you start mapping your location-based marketing strategy.

Defining Your Location-Based Marketing Goals

We would love to be able to tell you that because location-based marketing is full of cool technology it will magically solve all of your marketing problems. That would be like telling you that you'll find pots of gold at the end of the double rainbow.

This is still marketing and not magic. It is, however, fun stuff that can inspire you to do some very cool and creative things to target your audiences at the right time and place.

If you follow best marketing practices — which we assume you do — you'll start every campaign with a *strategic brief* (an overview of the situation). The brief describes important things like the product or service, the idea for the campaigns, the audience and its demographic breakdown (and perhaps some information on audience behavior), the challenges faced in making the idea come to life, the hurdles to overcoming the challenges, and the resources allocated. Just as in traditional marketing, starting with a brief is a good idea with location-based marketing.

Write your brief in reverse order. Start by asking yourself, "What do I want the audience to do?" Stating explicit goals for your campaign and location in your campaign allows you to create within a series of constraints:

- **Location:** This is a very broad topic, and constraining your team by what you want to achieve initially can help you decide what platforms are necessary to execute your campaign. In other words, platforms can often be determined by the constraints of the campaign.

- **Goals:** Base your goals on the kinds of activities you want to inspire. The most obvious goal is to get someone to check in to your establishment. But goals can be other things, like attaining a certain frequency of check-ins or number of times the mayorship changes hands during a campaign, specials unlocked, specials taken advantage of, items unlocked, or badges earned — and, of course, the revenue associated with the specials. We go much deeper into these in Chapter 11.

Location-based social networks can help you achieve any of the following things, all of which are worthwhile goals:

- Entice a new customer into your business.

- Reward someone with a prize or a badge.

- Create a competitive atmosphere for people around businesses they're passionate about.

- Build loyalty for a business or brand.

In the sections that follow, we tell you how to think through these goals when creating a strategic brief.

If you're not sure which location-based service to use for a campaign, you can test multiple providers to discover which service does the best for a certain type of campaign. The most important thing to remember with a test is that you should keep some variables constant across the test so you track the impact of changing a variable. Variables can include the platform, the offer, the location, the promotion money spent (yes, putting paid media behind a location-based campaign is essential), the frequency of earned media messages on Facebook, and the Twitter account used to promote the campaign.

Engaging your customer

LBS platforms identify people who are enthusiastic enough to say, "I am here." By *claiming* your venues on platforms, you get access to dashboards that give you a bird's-eye view of who is checking in to your location. We show you how to claim your location in Chapter 4. You can, through these dashboards, identify your prospects and customers and therefore engage your customers in an ongoing dialogue. Look at a participant's status, the frequency he checks in, and the content created.

Engagement is talking directly to a customer or prospect. When you engage with someone, there's a good chance you're creating brand loyalty. Think of engagement as the number of touch points you have with a group of people you care about, and then think about the quality of those engagements and whether they get you closer to your desired objective. The objective can be as simple as making potential customers aware that your business exists; it can also be a sale.

An LBS has ways to elevate the status of someone based on the fact that they have successfully checked into a place more times than another else. foursquare, Gowalla, and Yelp all have ways to recognize the one person who checks in to your business the most often. Figure 3-1 shows each of these platforms.

- ✔ foursquare calls this person the mayor and was the first to give a formal name to the person who checks in the most.
- ✔ Gowalla has a Leaderboard and lets you see who is in the lead.
- ✔ Yelp allows people to rule a group of places in a region, appointing each a Duke or Duchess.

These are people you want to engage. Ask them questions about what makes them want to check in to your business and find out if they recommend your business to others.

Another thing to pay attention to is the content that people create at your place. Most LBS pages let participants tell a bigger story than "I am here." Often, your supporters leave tips and recommendations that indicate what you are doing well and what they like about you. Other times, their feedback gives you the opportunity to learn about your downfalls and things that might keep people away.

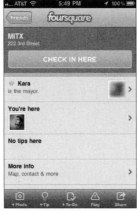  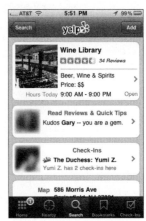

Figure 3-1:
You can
find the
person
who's
checked
in the most
on each
platform.

These people are the most important to engage, either to encourage their behavior or to show that you care enough to acknowledge the effort they took to give you feedback. Every complaint in social media is a chance to publicly turn a negative experience into a positive one. People who are willing to step up and criticize your business are often also willing to talk about the way that you righted a wrong, particularly if you do it in a noteworthy way.

Your venue or place page within a platform often contains tips, recommendations, pictures, and check-ins that you can use to find out who cares about your business and who would like to see you make improvements.

Building loyalty

There are several ways to use LBSs to build loyalty to your brand:

- **Tips and recommendations:** Many LBSs allow users to tell people what they like about a place via features called tips, highlights, or recommendations. These ideas are then propagated to users who are nearby, either by request or when they check in. These tips help customers form an impression of your business. When the participant taps the Tips icon, she sees tips left by past reviewers, as shown in Figure 3-2.

  You can leverage the tips and recommendations to promote your products and specials, but just because you can does not mean you should. Use the Amazon review approach. On Amazon, the brand is the least trusted when talking about its own product or service. People generally seek a third-party perspective, so anonymous users and friends are deemed far more trustworthy with people who are considering your product.

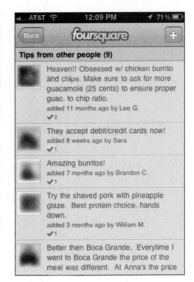

Figure 3-2:
Gain insight
about your
business
from tips.

As you get to know who the advocates are for your brand, you can give them some kind of incentive to help you with tips. For instance, AJ Bombers, a Milwaukee burger joint, offered a free cookie to anyone who posted a recommendation on foursquare.

✔ **Want lists:** A *want list* is a list of things that a user thinks will be good to do. These are created by perusing tips for places on either the web or smartphone. Figure 3-3 shows a place on foursquare that a user added on a want list. The place is "tagged" until the want is fulfilled.

This place is tagged.

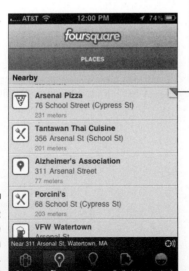

Figure 3-3:
This place
is tagged on
foursquare.

✔ **Pictures:** Pictures tell the story of your venue and can help a user decide whether to come to your place. Take pictures of things that are happening. Use pictures to do the following:

- *Demonstrate activity.* Show off how many people visit your business. If you're hosting an event, take lots of pictures to show people how awesome your store is. This will entice people to come in because they will want to be a part of the experience.

- *Show products.* Take pictures of your products so that people can see what they look like. This is particularly helpful if your product is not a commodity. Restaurants, for instance, have different takes on dishes. Applications like Foodspotting (http://www.foodspotting.com) and Instagram (http://instagr.am) can help showcase your products and also propagate the message to foursquare, Twitter, and Facebook. Figure 3-4 shows a photo posted on Instagram. SCVNGR is also particularly good at telling a story through pictures and challenges. Gowalla has picture-taking ability as well. Color uses a combination of picture, location, and the noise in the room to build a social graph for the user.

Consider uploading your own photos to see whether people are interested in following your stream, particularly on Instagram. For example, Great Divide Brewing uses YouTube and Facebook to demonstrate the brewing process and show happenings around the plant.

Figure 3-4:
Photos
posted in
Instagram
can be
integrated
into
foursquare.

- *Introduce staff.* This is a great opportunity to get people on a first-name basis with your staff. Because photos can accompany tips and highlights, you can post a picture of a staff member with a link to a Twitter account so people can converse before they ever get to your business. The more personal the touch, the more likely people are to make that connection that brings them into your store.

✔ **Specials and contests:** Specials and contests are great ways to get participants to check in to your business. Most LBS applications have ways to indicate that you have a special or contest happening.

Make sure that your special is truly special! You have to find the right mix of difficulty to achieve and majesty of the reward. If you try to convince people to compete to lead check-ins at your business for a free packet of ketchup on Saturdays, they aren't going to be very impressed. If you have people doing a series of challenges to find a key that could unlock free entrées once a week for a year, that might be worth doing.

The Holiday Deals Society

The Holiday Deals Society was built for the 2010 and early 2011 holiday season. Whrrl (which no longer exists) partnered with product makers like Philips, Hamilton Beach, Seagate, Elmer's, and Murphy USA. Those who checked in at Target, Best Buy, and Walmart were eligible for prizes, including Norelco razors (Mike won one when he checked in at Best Buy), Sonicare electric toothbrushes, Philips flexible-fit earhook headphones, Elmer's Glue memory-making gift bags, Hamilton Beach slow cookers, Seagate GoFlex USB drives, and Murphy USA coupons.

This was a very large scale effort, but demonstrated the power of an LBS. Whrrl had near a million users and was able to get major engagement and usage without having the largest audience in the field. It partnered with big brands and gave away things worth playing for. The game was simple. You checked into one of the partnering retail stores and got a virtual scratch ticket. You played the game and it would tell you if you won. You could play daily. Once you played, you then had an opportunity to act on other recommendations for better shopping experiences at the stores.

The program had 1,500 members after two-and-a-half weeks with over 19,000 actions taken. The actions included posting check-ins and prizes to Twitter and Facebook as well as playing the game to win prizes. Forty-four percent of the people acted on at least one recommendation and each person who did so told their friends to do what they just did an average of 3.3 times. Seventy five thousand people viewed recommendations in total.

This campaign was largely focused on engagement, without a tie-in to sales. Putting the sales data together with the results is the end goal, but most point-of-sale systems aren't sophisticated enough to push a customer's data to any system. The goal of many LBS campaigns is to get people into the store.

There is an important distinction between seeding loyalty with location-based services (the subject of this section) and incorporating LBSs into a formal loyalty campaign. We talk about the latter in Chapter 7.

Conducting customer research

You see a lot of people talking about your brand on location-based services. So what do you do with that information?

If you're a friend of a customer or prospect, you have access to the footfeed of that customer. The *footfeed* (not to be confused with the check-in aggregator with the same name) is the log of places that a person has checked in to, and it gives you a sense of what kinds of businesses your customers like and how often they frequent them. If you know that one of your customers likes your competitor down the street, ask him why he likes the other business, and you can find ways to improve your business.

Aligning Your Goals to a Platform

Each platform has its strengths and weaknesses, and understanding the platforms allows you to pick the right platform for a campaign or tailor your marketing campaign around a platform.

The relatively low cost (for now) to use these platforms means you can test a campaign on multiple platforms.

Here are some possible goals for a campaign:

✔ **You want to build brand awareness.**

Your goal is to make people aware of what your business does, what your brand stands for, what products you sell, and how and when to engage you. Building awareness of your brand is the first step in getting to the even more coveted consideration, which can lead to a purchase. Facebook Places, Yelp, and foursquare have the largest audiences. Gowalla and SCVNGR have great ways to template the experience via trips and treks. WHERE taps into an advertising network. These can all help build awareness in different ways. Awareness is a tricky animal and most of the platforms in the book can give you a further boost.

✔ **You want advocacy.**

The days when people listened strictly to marketing are fading away. People trust other people more than they trust the ad purchased by the company who made the product, bought the time, and created the TV spot, banner ad, or clutter buster.

Think of Amazon. It mastered the art of the review, and other companies have followed suit. Social media and location-based platforms create the same kinds of advocacy and allow people to spread the love beyond the platform into others where they may have more people who care about the message they want to spread. Most social networks allow a user to push a check in to other services. For examples, Foodspotting allows cross-posting to Facebook, foursquare, flickr, and Twitter, as shown in Figure 3-5. foursquare and Gowalla are the best for building advocacy due to their tips and highlights features.

✔ **You want to acquire customers.**

Offers that bring new customers into the store provide short-term gains for your business at potentially smaller profit margins, but they can also build short-term advocacy, awareness, and hopefully convince customers to return. Location-based marketing allows you to cast a smaller net to catch the people who will take advantage of your offer. SCVNGR, foursquare, Facebook Places, Loopt, WHERE, and Yelp all have different types of offers that you can use to get people in the door.

Here's an example of how you can use location-based marketing to acquire customers: The Sports Authority ran a foursquare promotion on Black Friday to get more customers into the store. If a customer checked in and cross-posted to Twitter, the customer entered a drawing to win a $500 gift card. Because the end goal was to draw more customers, the winner had to be present to win. The Sports Authority also had a very good special for the mayor: a $10 coupon to use with any purchase.

Figure 3-5: Foodspotting allows customers to tell others they're at your place with Twitter and Facebook, as well.

✔ **You want to seed loyalty.**

Whether you actually already have a loyalty program, location-based services can play a significant role in loyalty initiatives. If you look at the root of loyalty, a brand becomes something that customers connect to on a level where they want to repeat the experience. A loyalist is steadfast in allegiance and/or duty. In this case, think of *allegiance* as advocating your brand by telling friends and family about its virtues. You can think of *duty* as purchasing and repurchasing the product. Check-ins, specials, pictures, badges, pins, and so on give people more ways to interact with and spread the message of your brand. See Chapter 6 for more information on this topic.

foursquare is the leader in loyalty. There are a number of platforms that plug into foursquare to leverage the data to give rewards. American Express has a program that allows a customer to attach a card to a foursquare account. foursquare also has loyalty programs with Tasti D-Lite and Vons that give coupons and rewards.

✔ **You want to find out more about your audience.**

Learning more about your customers and prospects may be the best reason to participate in the LBS movement. Knowing where your customers go and when they go there can help you tailor campaigns to change their behavior. Gowalla is the most open of the applications. You can get public check-in information for most venues just by having a Gowalla account. This information is personally identifiable, and you can map it directly back to a Gowalla account.

Creating Programs Built for Minimum Interaction

With 500 million Facebook users and counting and several million on foursquare, LBSs still 'haven't achieved mainstream penetration. If you make your campaign minimally intrusive to the user, you can help encourage participation. Make your specials or contests:

✔ **Easy to use:** Don't make your special too complex. Make sure that the terms of engagement are easy enough for someone who's never used a location-based service before.

✔ **Rewarding:** If your special isn't special enough, no one will want it. Costs are minimal for specials and prizes, but it still takes time and effort to build your campaign.

If you want an example of a service that offers great rewards, check out Groupon (www.groupon.com). Groupon is a service that offers users a local, daily deal. It is a minimally invasive service that sends an e-mail once a day to find out if users would like to participate in the deal. If the deal hits a minimum threshold of participation, then the deal is on. If it does not, then there is no deal. This allows you to control your costs and be ensured that you have a certain amount of participation before the deal is executed. The reason that people love Groupon is that the deals are awesome — most of them are 50 percent off, and some are even 90 percent off.

✔ **Available to as many people as possible:** Specials for the person with the most frequent check-ins (called the mayor, ambassador, and so on depending on the platform) are commonplace. But consider making an LBS available to as many people as possible. Instead of limiting your specials to the mayor, give everyone a chance to get in on the deal. foursquare now has a wide array of specials that make specials both interesting and worthwhile:

- *Flash* specials appear only at certain times.

- *Swarm* specials are activated when a certain number of people check in at the same time.

- *Friends* specials are activated when a party of friends check in together.

- *Newbie* specials only activate the first time someone checks in.

- *Check-in* specials are unlocked whenever anyone checks in.

Invoke the Ben & Jerry's Rule, which is that the special must be awesome, everyone must be able to participate, and the mayor should get something for being the mayor. Here's how the offer excels at involving as many people as possible:

- *It's a good deal.* The deal is three scoops for $3. The normal price for three scoops of Ben & Jerry's is around $5, which makes the offer a good deal.

- *Everyone can participate.* You just need to be on foursquare and check in at Ben & Jerry's.

- *Being the mayor is worth it.* The mayor gets a free scoop — icing on the cake!

National hamburger chain Rally's (which is also called Checkers and Snaps, depending on the location) uses this same principle: It offers a free small milkshake on every third foursquare check-in. The mayor gets one every visit.

Choosing a Platform for the Short or Long Term

The quick, nimble, and lightweight nature of an LBS encourages you to experiment with social media engagement and customer acquisition. When you've proven the value of a one time offer (one-off), you can involve LBSs in more than a single, one-off tactic in your campaign. One-offs are typically test runs and usually are used as a learning tool. They can give you a sense whether it's worth creating a larger campaign off. See Chapter 10 for more detail on campaign effectiveness.

Ultimately, you have to decide what is meaningful to you. If you want LBSs to be meaningful to your organization, you have to think about it as a part of every one of your campaigns. Ask what the location components are and how location fits into a campaign. For a longer-term view, consider the costs, setup time, and functionality of the platform.

Return should always outweigh your investment. After you determine the critical path for setting up a campaign (see Chapter 5 about setting up a campaign), you can trim your setup costs.

Some platforms are set up to work with you long term and allow you to plug into tool kits so that you can build any campaign you can dream up. foursquare is into loyalty campaigns, SCVNGR is the backbone for a Smithsonian exploration tool, and DoubleDutch is fundamental to Cincinnati's Porkappolis program and the University of Arizona's exploration campaign.

Most platforms come with an application programming interface (API), which allows you to use the functionality of a platform to create new applications. Here are some APIs to look into:

- Many companies use the **foursquare** (http://developer. foursquare.com) API for complex campaigns.

  The API allows you quick access to users, venues, check-ins, tips, and photos.

- The **SCVNGR** (http://scvngr.com/pricing) API comes with a fee — but it's quite powerful, so you may find it worth the price.

  There are several tiers of service that are based on your usage per month. You can create custom challenges, treks, and rewards for between $80 (for a capacity of 15) and $1,080 (for a capacity of 100) per month. You get the ability to create 5 challenges for free.

- **Gowalla** also has an API that you can find at http://gowalla.com/ api/docs/oauth.

Sending users on a scavenger hunt for rewards

Boston based SCVNGR teamed up with *The Boston Globe* to send users on a series of scavenger hunts or treks through Boston. Challenges were related to romance, movies, sports, technology, photography, and news in Boston. Winners won these prizes:

✓ Red Sox Tickets: A pair of Green Monster tickets for a September game

✓ A romantic gondola ride for two on the Charles River

✓ Two Showcase Cinema de Lux tickets to the movie of your choice, plus a $30 concessions voucher

✓ A $50 Apple iTunes gift card

✓ Beantown Excursion: A four-pack of tickets for the Beantown Trolley and the Pru's Skywalk Observatory this September

✓ A $50 gift card to treat yourself to something special!

Presenting Timely Deals, Offers, and Content

The great thing about LBS is that you can leverage the attributes of a particular place — and, in the case of platforms like Google Places, Bizzy, and WHERE, past check-ins, preferences, wants, and recommendations — to give users something that is customized to them. You can make your deals, offers, and content timely and relevant in several ways:

✓ **Lock down location to present hyper-targeted deals.**

LBSs give you a person's location, as well as an aggregate view of where a person likes to go. One way to get an aggregate view is to create applications that are applicable in only certain locations. For example, building a mobile commerce checkout application using AisleBuyer allows you to know exactly where customers are in your store. The application allows users to scan an item to get prices and details, build an *in-store* shopping cart, and even check out without going to the register. You can give customers deals on the items they scan or chances to win their entire cart!

✓ **Cast a wider net with location-based circular-style applications.**

Some applications, like shopkick, essentially act like a store circular (a branded, mini-newspaper that advertises current deals for a particular store). For instance, shopkick tells a customer about all the deals in your store. Customers earn points for checking into products. shopkick is designed to get people to explore products in the store and rewards them for doing so.

✔ **Use recommendations and tips to enhance your business profile.**

You can include tips about your own business — but beware of appearing self-serving if you do so. We recommend considering opportunities to leave messages that enhance the experiences of people who see your message.

Hugo Boss is a brand that is about modern style and elegance, and the company uses tips in a unique way. Hugo Boss has aligned itself with New York City's finest museums, its foursquare profile page (`www.foursquare.com/hugoboss`), as shown in Figure 3-6, includes a contest and tips about various museums in New York. The tips tell you how to find winning works of the Hugo Boss Prize, an award given every two years to recognize contemporary artists.

✔ **Use reviews and blog posts to increase content longevity.**

Check out the reviews on services like Yelp (`http://www.yelp.com`) and Chowhound (`http://chowhound.com`). Yelpers write detailed reviews about their experiences.

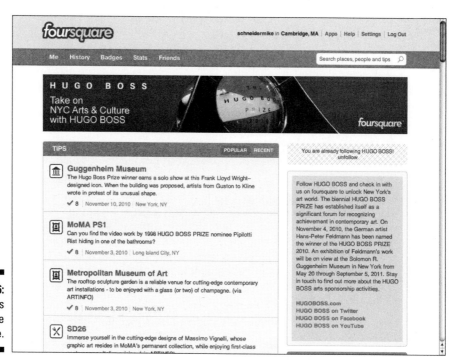

Figure 3-6:
Hugo Boss's
foursquare
page.

✔ **Create contextual offers that bring people to your location.**

Your ultimate goal is to get a person's data and make very smart recommendations that the participant will like, resulting in a sale.

Whrrl's Society Rewards program was the closest to being able to do this. The program allowed companies to put contests and recommendations in the path of people who are attached to a particular Society, which (in Yelp) is a group of people brought together by a common interest. You could attach a prize to a Society, and you had a better chance of targeting someone who would care about the reward and, hopefully, your business.

Halls wanted to use WHERE to drive cough drop sales. WHERE used its dynamic targeting abilities to target regions that scored high on the flu index. WHERE used geofencing technology to serve the offer to people near CVS, Walgreens and Walmart locations. The campaign outperformed a similar static campaign by 62 percent. The static campaign served the offer to people no matter their flu index score and no matter their location. They found that proximity to the drug store and a higher propensity to be sick increased the call to action significantly.

McDonald's wanted to test the context that place applies to see if proximity to the restaurant made people more likely to look at their offer. Average click-through for banner ads is around .02 percent. Targeting people who were near McDonald's and telling them how close the nearest one yielded a .92 percent click through rate. Click through rates are low, but if you look at the percent increase, it is very significant (4500 percent).

Chapter 4

Checking In and Playing the Game

· ·

In This Chapter

▶ Searching for your business

▶ Finding and claiming your venues

▶ Checking out what goes into good offers

· ·

*W*hile most users of location-based services use these services for fun and entertainment, they like getting value from it as well. To that end, it's important that you understand how to successfully "play the game." This includes things like finding and claiming your current location(s), understanding the importance of a first-time check-in experience, knowing who is checking in, and ultimately recognizing the power of a participant becoming the leading "checker-inner" at a location.

In the context of location-based services, *location* is a latitude and longitude coordinate. *Place* and *venue* are a set of coordinates (or locations) that have a set of attributes, such as a business type, name, street address, and more. Technically there is a difference between a location, place, and point of interest, but we use *location* to mean location and *venue* and *place* to mean place or point of interest.

Searching for Your Business

A lot of times, you'll find a place has already been created for your business. Each location-based service needs to maintain a database of places. They're created in a variety of ways, including these:

- ✓ **From the Internet:** Some, like Google Places, are created by combing the Internet for addresses. AT&T's YP.com was created from the yellow pages.

- ✓ **From users that use the service:** Some of these place databases were created from scratch. Users create pages as they check in. This is why Gowalla and foursquare's databases are sometimes missing places. If someone hasn't created a page for your business, you may not find one. You also may find multiple pages, with slightly different names.

You'll want to search for your business on the LBS that you choose to go with and claim those places so that you can create specials and, most importantly, get access to dashboards that tell you who is checking in to your business. You will also be able to *standardize* (declare the proper format) the name of your venue. For example, Hannaford's, Hannaford Bros, Hannaford Brothers, Hannaford can all be combined with Hannaford.

Claiming your page doesn't prevent someone else from creating a new place, but it lowers the chance of that happening. Most platforms are working on ensuring that that does not happen.

If you're claiming your location using an app on your mobile device, your place may not appear on the list of nearby places. Sometimes less popular venues — and by less popular, we mean "less frequently checked in to" — won't pop up immediately on the 10–15 suggested places. You may be in a densely populated area with a lot of businesses, and your app only shows some of the venues in the area. If your business doesn't show up, you have to manually search for your business. Keep this difficulty in mind, because customers may have the same problem checking in to your business.

Start by finding your location on the service(s) that you select. Figure 4-1 shows a search on foursquare for the arts and crafts supply chain Hobby Lobby. Several venues appear with the accompanying details.

Users ultimately have control over the places that are created. Keep an eye out for places within your place (men's room, the bar, the video games department). You may have some active folks checking in here that you will want to embrace. If a person gets so inspired, they can create the pinball machine in your bar as a place, the sink in the ladies room, or even the moose head on the wall.

Figure 4-1:
Searching
venues on
foursquare.

foursquare	Aaron in Austin, TX Apps Help Settings Log Out

Me   History   Badges   Stats   Friends   Search places, people and tips

Search

Search for venues, tips, people or venue tags below. Narrow down your search with a location in the "near" field.

Results for	Near	
hobby lobby	Austin, TX	Search

☐ Sort venues by distance only

Venues (37)   Tips (2)   People (0)   Tags (0)

☒ **Hobby Lobby**
4040 South Lamar Blvd
Austin, TX 78704
♥ 3 tips
♥ 492 check-ins

☒ **Hobby Lobby**
7950 Research Blvd
Lamar Blvd.
Austin, TX 78758
♥ 2 tips
♥ 328 check-ins

Finding and Claiming Your Place

One of the first things you need to determine when setting up a location-based marketing program is which location-based service or services you want to use. (We discuss choosing an LBS service in Chapter 3.) If a lot of customers or potential customers use a particular service, that's one you should definitely claim.

Scan through 5–10 of these services, because, depending on your venue, you may find that your customers have gravitated toward a particular LBS already. For example, in North Carolina, TriOut has a disproportionate number of followers, as that' is where the service is based.

One of the most important steps in setting up your location-based marketing campaign is *claiming your place,* which means that you need to go through the LBS process to own your business's place page in their system. This gives you privileges like access to the dashboard and the ability to create specials. This process varies from service to service, as we discuss in the sections that follow.

You must set up an account for any of the services that you plan to use as part of your location-based marketing initiative. With some services, you can use a personal account. In the case of Yelp, SCVNGR, and Facebook Places, a business account is required.

Set up an account for either the owner of the business or the individual(s) who will be claiming, monitoring, and/or marketing using LBSs. In the latter case, particularly at a large business, a process should be established to facilitate multiple access points, so an e-mail convention like `info@company name.com` — where all employees involved with the LBS can access that e-mail account — might be best.

You might have duplicate entries for your store or stores, which are *venues* or *places*. You'll have to request that these places be consolidated. All of the data, unique visitors, check-ins, and tips are aggregated and you eliminate the "which place do I check into?" question.

Note that the claiming process usually takes between two days and a week. If you're claiming more than one venue with multiple places, be prepared to go through a different vetting process depending on which service you choose; it may take more time.

Because location-based services are free to use, go ahead and sign up for as many as you like. Then you can experiment to find the one you and your customers have the most success with.

After setting up your account(s), you can start searching the location-based service(s) and staking your claim. In the sections that follow, we tell you how to claim your business with the most popular location-based services. On some services, you can use your smartphone to do this, but on many it will be easier to do it on the web, particularly if you need to claim multiple venues. In Chapter 5, we tell you how to add your business to those services if it isn't already included, as well as how to refine your profile with those services.

Yelp

When you claim your business on Yelp, you gain a lot of administrative capabilities. You can edit business info without waiting for Yelp's approval, view page analytics, message customers, run advertisements, and more.

The claiming process is straightforward. Just remember that Yelp requires you to use a business account, not a personal account. Here's how to get started on Yelp:

Follow these steps to claim your page on Yelp:

1. **Go to http://yelp.com.**

2. **Search for your business name.**

   You may need to specify the city and state where your business is located.

3. **Click the title of your venue in the search results.**

   Your business page appears. If it's unclaimed, you see a red Claim This Business button at the bottom of the page, as shown in Figure 4-2.

4. **Click the Claim This Business button.**

   The next page shows a set of instructions. Yelp is different from many other LBS networks because it doesn't link managerial claims to a personal account. You'll create a dedicated business account on Yelp in the next step of the claim process.

5. **Click the Go to Step 1 button.**

   On this page, you create a business account, shown in Figure 4-3. If you already have a business account, click the "Log in here to add a business" link and skip to Step 7.

6. **Fill out the form (name, e-mail address, and password) and click the Continue button.**

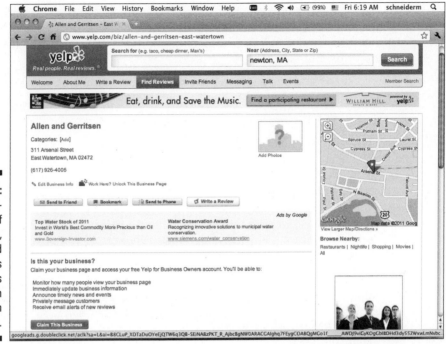

Figure 4-2:
Your busi-
ness, if
unclaimed,
has a red
Claim This
Business
button on
the bottom
of the page.

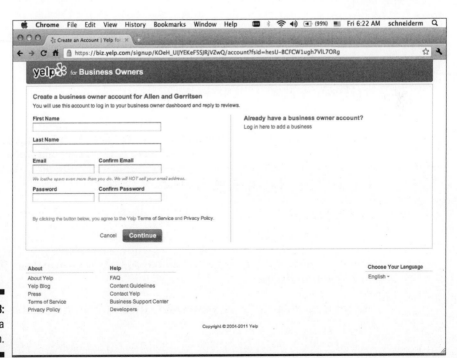

Figure 4-3:
Fill out a
simple form.

Next you will need to verify your authority to administer the page via phone confirmation. Take note of the verification code; you'll need it to claim.

7. Enter or correct your phone number, and then click the Call Me Now button.

Remember to add an extension if you' use an automated voice system.

8. Answer the phone call and enter the verification code appearing on your screen.

Your claim is now complete.

foursquare

On foursquare, you can claim an individual venue or a chain of venues. If your brand doesn't have physical locations to claim, you can create a brand page, which allows users to leave tips at foursquare locations.

To claim a venue on foursquare, you must have a foursquare user profile, and foursquare grants you administrative permission to your venue through that profile. After your venue has been claimed, you can sign in to your user profile to see that you're listed as a manager of your venues, and can therefore claim your venue.

Managerial access gives you the ability to add foursquare users as employees or fellow managers. Employees and managers of venues (if labeled as such in the foursquare database) are ineligible to achieve mayor status at those venues. So if your mayor is one of your employees (as is the case with many unclaimed venues), you can appoint that person an employee within foursquare so that he or she can continue to check in, but surrender the mayor status to one of your customers.

foursquare is constantly changing and evolving. By the time you read this book, the developers at foursquare may have made some changes to the claim process. If you need help with the claiming process, foursquare has a robust support service you can access at `http://support.foursquare.com`.

Claiming venues

If the venue is one of a kind, you can claim it individually. If you have fewer than ten venues to claim, you can also claim those individually. To claim an individual venue, start at `http://foursquare.com` on your web browser and follow these steps:

1. Enter the name of your venue and city in the search box.

2. **Click your venue title in the search results.**

   At the bottom of the right column on the venue page, there should be a question that asks "Do you manage this venue?" followed by a Claim Here link. Look closely. It is teeny-tiny. See Figure 4-4.

3. **Click the Claim Here link.**

   A page opens, where you can verify the business you're claiming.

4. **Click the Continue Claiming This Venue link.**

   foursquare will ask you again if you're authorized to claim the venue.

5. **(Optional) Read the Venue Platform Terms of Use.**

6. **Click Yes.**

   foursquare reminds you that your venue page will be linked to your personal account. If you're a small business with a few venues or less, that shouldn't be a problem. However, if you have a lot of locations to claim, you should probably create a separate user account that's dedicated to managing the venues.

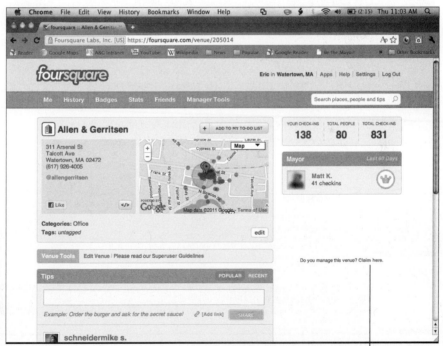

Figure 4-4:
The venue page for Allen & Gerritsen.

Click this link to claim your venue.

Next, you're taken to a page that asks what kind of venue you're claiming. See Figure 4-5.

7. **Click the link appropriate to the venue you're claiming:**

   If you have ten or more venues, you may process a bulk claim, which we cover in the next section of this chapter.

   • *One of a kind:* You can get a verification code via phone.

   • *Chain with less than 10 venues:* If you're a chain with fewer than 10 venues, you claim those venues in the same way individual venues are claimed.

   • *Chain with 10 or more venues:* Fill in the form to open a ticket with foursquare support. (See Figure 4-6.) Make sure you include *BULK* in the title of your ticket. We talk more about finishing the claiming process in the next section.

8. **Note the verification code when foursquare gives it to you.**

9. **Enter your verification code.**

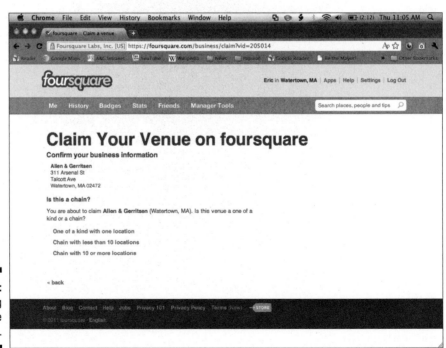

Figure 4-5:
Claiming
multiple
venues.

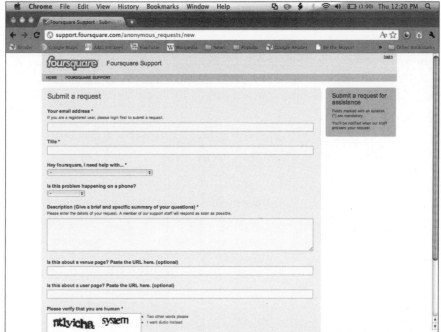

Claiming a chain

After you submit your ticket, a foursquare representative will e-mail you, verify that you have authority to claim the venues you want to claim, and send you an Excel spreadsheet. You'll be asked for these two pieces of information:

- ✔ The name of the foursquare user URL that will be the administrator for the locations (Remember, you may want to create a new user profile solely for this purpose.)

  A user URL looks like this: `https://foursquare.com/user/#######`.

- ✔ A list of the foursquare venue URLs for the locations you want to claim.

  foursquare venue URLs look like this: `https://foursquare.com/venue/######`.

foursquare is pretty responsive to bulk claims. Check back on your user profile a few days or even a few hours later to see the venues you can manage.

Creating a brand page

You may not have physical venues to claim within the foursquare database but still want to interact with your customers, viewers, or followers in the location-based space. A great way to do that on foursquare is to create a brand page. Brand pages can leave tips at foursquare venues, and, unlike user pages, they don't have a cap on how many people can follow them.

Check out other branded pages in foursquare's pages gallery at `https://foursquare.com/pages`. Figure 4-7 shows the branded page for the Bravo Channel. To get started with a brand page, go to `http://foursquare.com/business` and click the Learn More link in the Brands section.

Figure 4-7: The Bravo page on foursquare shows how a brand can use location-based services.

You'll be taken to a landing page that explains more about brand pages. Click the Next button at the bottom of the screen to start creating your brand page. Download the Excel spreadsheet. Fill out the form and e-mail it to `partners@foursquare.com`.

To create a brand page, you will need these four things:

✔ A foursquare user URL that is connected to a brand Twitter account.

Your foursquare user URL should look like this: `http://foursquare.com/yourbrandname`.

✔ A two- or three-sentence description of your brand complete with any relevant social media links.

Write this description using HTML. It speeds up the process of your request.

✔ An 860 x 130-pixel banner image that includes the word "foursquare" or a foursquare logo. Many brands like to add a catchy tagline to their banner images about what followers can expect when they follow the brand.

✔ A 185 x 185-pixel logo at 72dpi (dots per inch) to be included in foursquare's page gallery.

You can change your foursquare user URL to match your Twitter name by authorizing your Twitter account through the foursquare website.

Gowalla

When you claim your business on Gowalla, you can edit your business's profile details, add a check-in message, or even feature your venue with a custom stamp. To claim your page, follow these steps:

1. **Go to http://gowalla.com/business.**

2. **Search for your business.**

3. **Click your business's link in the search results.**

4. **Click the button that says, "Do you run this place? Claim it now."**

   The button is underneath the map on the right side of your business page. See Figure 4-8.

5. **Fill in the claiming form.**

   You need your business's address, phone number, and other business links from Yelp or Google Places.

6. **Click the Submit button.**

   You will immediately receive a phone call — a recording of a pleasant Australian man. He will give you the confirmation code.

7. **Note the confirmation code and enter it in the box.**

   You may have to wait a few days before the processing is complete, but after that your user account will have manager control over your venue.

After your request has been approved, you receive an e-mail notification to the e-mail address you used to sign up for Gowalla.

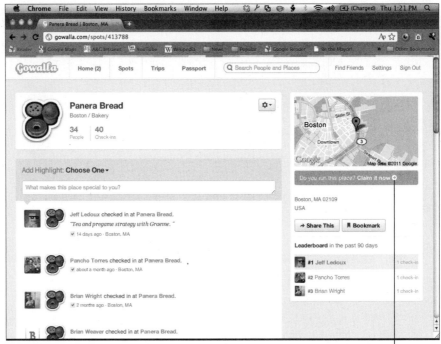

Figure 4-8:
Click the big green button to claim your venue.

Click this button to claim your venue.

Facebook Places

Claiming a business on Facebook allows you to add check-in deals for your visitors as well as merge your Facebook Places Page with your Facebook Fan Page. Follow these steps:

1. **Go to www.facebook.com.**

2. **In the search box at the top of the page, search for your business's name.**

3. **Choose your venue from the Facebook Place Pages results.**

4. **On the venue page, click the Is This Your Business link at the bottom of the left column.**

    A window appears asking if you have the authority to claim this business page. See Figure 4-9.

5. **Select the "I certify I am an official representative of *your business*" option.**

    A new pop-up window appears; see Figure 4-10.

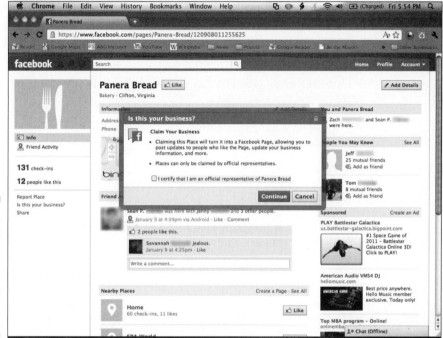

Figure 4-9:
Facebook
asks if this
is indeed
your busi-
ness. That
begins the
process.

Figure 4-10:
Confirm
your phone
number with
Facebook.

6. **Ensure that the phone number listed on the venue is correct.**

   If you can be reached at an extension, enter the extension line into the domain in this window.

7. **Click the Call Me Now button.**

8. **Enter the code given to you over the phone in the domain.**

9. **Click the Verify button.**

   You get an e-mail notification that your request to claim your venue in Facebook Places has been approved.

Google Places

Because one in three Google searches are conducted with local intent and Google Places Pages are prominently displayed in Google results, claiming your Google Places Page is vital to your online marketing. When you claim your Google Places page, you can optimize the information on your page, such as address, hours of operation, payment method accepted and more. You can also purchase Google Boost, which gives your venue page a leg up in search results. Finally, you get access to robust analytics that tell you how many people are coming to your venue page, where they're coming from, and how many are clicking through to your website.

To claim your business on Google Places, follow these steps:

1. **Go to `http://maps.google.com`.**

2. **Search for your business name.**

   You may need to add your town and state to find your exact venue.

3. **When you've found your business on the map, click the small red pin that represents your business.**

   A window will appear with some basic information about your business.

4. **Click the More Info link.**

   The next page is a Google Places Page. See Figure 4-11.

Click this link to edit your page.

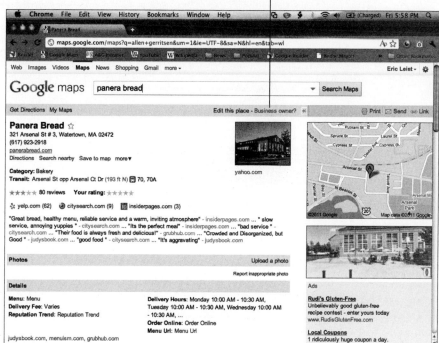

5. **Click the Business Owner? link.**

   The next page gives you three options: Edit My Business Information, Suspend This Listing, and This Isn't My Listing.

6. **Select the Edit My Business Information option and click the Continue button at the bottom of the page.**

7. **Select the method by which you would like to verify that you are a manager at the business and click Finish.**

8. **Note the PIN number and enter it in your Google Places dashboard to finish your claim; see Figure 4-12.**

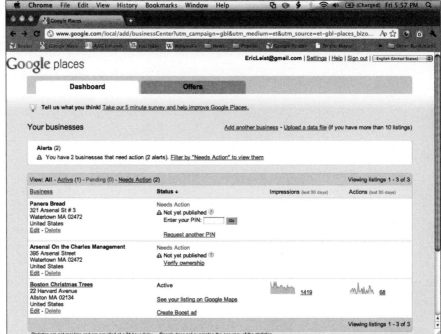

Figure 4-12:
Finish the
Google
claiming
process.

Checking Out Appealing Offers

Your goal is to have a potential customer check in to one of your locations to be wowed rather than underwhelmed by the experience. To accomplish this, you need a location that is rich with comments and content (photos, reviews, tips, and so on) in addition to an exciting offer.

Start thinking about what to offer your customers early and often. Having a strong offer is key to encouraging future check-ins. Offers don't need to be monetary but should make your customers feel special. You get only one chance to make a first impression. We talk more about the creating the right offer in Chapter 6.

A local theater in Austin, The Hideout, takes a smart approach with its four-square check-ins by providing a "two for the price of one" admission on a participant's first, 5th, or 10th visit, and *free* admission for the mayor. As you can see in Figure 4-13, this offer can be unlocked any time a participant checks in. This type of offer is not only compelling to first-time check-ins but also the mayor (free admission) and for subsequent check-ins.

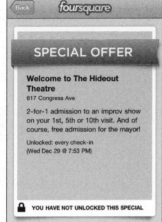

Figure 4-13:
An engaging
offer from
The Hideout
Theatre in
Austin, TX.

Depending on the LBS you're using, the name of the title for the person who checks in the most varies from mayor (foursquare) to Duke or Duchess (Yelp). Most LBSs let you know who's checked in the most, as shown in Figure 4-14.

Figure 4-14:
Checking
out who is
checked in
to your
location.

With several of the services, you can even comment on your customers' check-ins. This experience helps strengthen the bond between your business and your customer.

Widening and *tiering* (creating different offers for different stages) your offers to those beyond just the person who checks in the most can help mitigate any frustration or ensuing apathy for those customers who aren't leading the pack in check-ins.

Here are the other benefits of tiering your offers:

✔ **It encourages active check-ins.**

This starts with good old-fashioned marketing, letting people know that you're participating in a particular location-based service by announcing it on your signage, collateral, menus, and via the training of your staff. Let customers know that you care about their check-ins and reward their check-ins via offers or specials, which get better the more often they check in.

✔ **It offers users benefits to check in.**

Find out which companies, restaurants, and bars do a good job at welcoming customers. Which stores have strong offers? Which acknowledge their most-frequent visitors by featuring them on the wall (or in the case of Figure 4-15, offering them their own parking spot)?

Figure 4-15: This business takes its foursquare mayorship very seriously.

✔ **It gives you the benefits of a check-in.**

You learn quite a bit about your customers, such as what offers they use and what other places they frequent.

✔ **It creates a good post–check-in experience.**

Think about what keeps customers coming back.

A few things to keep in mind as you are designing your location-based marketing program:

✔ Would you check in again to your location? While it's always dangerous to form a "focus group of one," nobody knows your business better than you. Is your experience as good as other memorable experiences?

✔ Like an online community or a successful Facebook Page, it's important to foster conversation. This can come from you, or you can (and should) encourage your customers to contribute.

✔ Actively recognize your customers and, in particular, your most-frequent visitors. You would be amazed at what hanging their picture on your wall can do for their loyalty.

✔ While not all of the LBS services currently allow you to create your own *icons* or *badges* (which are custom ways to identify yourself and your rewards in the application), this aspect is sure to catch on more as these services evolve. We talk more about badges and rewards in Chapter 6, but for now, it's key to understand the importance of the "gaming" aspect of location-based services. While not everyone wants to (or will) use LBS for the gaming factor, a lot of people spend time earning points, badges, and virtual goods. The good thing about these types of incentives is that they are either free or relatively inexpensive.

While foursquare allows for certain custom badges to be created by larger programs, you can always look to services that allow you to create custom challenges — like SCVNGR. In some cases, Gowalla will create custom virtual goods, like they've done for local Austin companies One Taco and Sweet Leaf Tea, which can be redeemed for real-world equivalents.

Disney inks a deal with Gowalla

Disney has a deal with Gowalla that provides virtual pins at all of their Disneyland Resort and Walt Disney World Resort theme parks. What's brilliant about this for anyone that's visited the Magic Kingdom before is that collectible pins (physical ones) are all the rage. Now parents and their kids can collect elegant virtual pins, which I imagine some day will be capable of being traded and shared. You can see some of the more popular pins from the Disney/Gowalla collection shown in the following figure.

Check In at Disney Parks with Gowalla

posted on November 18th, 2010 by Thomas Smith, Social Media Director, Disney Parks

Part II
Location-Based Marketing in Action

The 5th Wave   By Rich Tennant

"Tell the boss you-know-who is trashing him on Yelp again."

In this part . . .

*I*t's time to dive into the "marketing" part of the book. If you're interested in location-based marketing, this is probably the most important part of the book. In this part, we cover

- ✔ The nuts and bolts of a location-based marketing campaign
- ✔ How to create and test a great offer (or offers)
- ✔ Using location-based services to create a loyalty program

Chapter 5

Building a Location-Based Marketing Campaign

As a marketer, you probably find creating marketing campaigns routine; a location-based marketing campaign isn't that different.

Of course, any good campaign starts with a goal, and you should know what your goals are for general planning and budgeting purposes. If you haven't made your goals yet, turn to Chapter 3 to do so.

Ultimately, understanding what you're trying to do with a specific campaign — even if it includes multiple goals — can make it easier to plan, set up, measure, and judge whether your campaign was a success.

Diving in head first to "try" location-based services probably isn't the best use of your time. That's not to say that you can't learn a thing or two through trial and error, but think about what would happen if one day you just started randomly e-mailing people asking them to come into your store. It might be semi-effective, but you also would've wasted a lot of time and would have no idea if you were successful.

As we discuss in Chapter 3, picking a service provider is one of the first things you should consider when getting started. This should ultimately fall in line with goal(s) you're trying to accomplish, but unless you think you're leaning toward a scavenger hunt type of experience (which isn't the worst idea in the world) or you already have a lot of equity in your Yelp presence (which many restaurants and small businesses do), it's probably easier to get started by using foursquare and/or Gowalla.

Throughout this chapter, we tell you how to create your venue page to meet those goals, execute against those goals, measure those goals and finally, to ensure that your business is ready to interact with customers once they decided to engage with you.

Creating Your Venue

If your business doesn't have a page set up on your LBS of choice, you can set up your venue. After your venue is set up, you can then claim it. (See Chapter 4.)

Whether you have one or multiple venues, you can go ahead and follow the steps here. However, if you work with more than ten venues, the rules for claiming your venue will vary depending on the LBS you're using.

foursquare

If your search for your venue was unsuccessful on foursquare, follow these steps to set up your venue. *Note:* The information you can include when you're working with your computer's web browser is slightly different from what you can include when you're using a smartphone or tablet, as you can see in the steps that follow. One significant difference is that you can geotag your venue if you're using your smartphone or tablet.

1. **Go to `http://foursquare.com` (or use the app on your smartphone).**

2. **Search for your company's name in the search box.**

3. **Click the Add a New Venue to foursquare link.**

4. **Add your venue information.**

   On the web version, you provide the following information:

   • *Venue name*

   • *Venue street address*

   • *Cross street (optional)*

- *City, state, and postal code*
- *Twitter handle*
- *Venue phone number*
- *Category*

On your smartphone or tablet, you provide the following information:

- *Venue name*
- *Category*
- *Venue street address* (You need to do this only if the geotagging on your smartphone misplaces your venue on the map or when you want to add a cross street.)

5. **Click Add Venue or Add to create your location.**

Gowalla

When this book went to press, you could create a venue — or *spot,* to use Gowalla's terminology — using *only* a smartphone or tablet, so go to the Gowalla app on your smartphone or tablet and follow these steps:

1. **Search for your company's name in search box.**

2. **Tap the + button in the top-right corner of your screen.**

3. **Enter the name of your spot (venue).**

4. **Tap Next Step and enter a description of your spot.**

5. **Choose a category.**

   These include choices like "Architecture & Buildings," "Event," "Food," and "Travel & Lodging," among several others.

   If you can't determine a category that you fit into, select the one that most closest fits your needs and expand on who you are in your description (touch Back to go back to that step).

6. **If the location of your venue looks correct on the map, go to step 7. If your venue is in the wrong place, reposition its location by dragging and dropping the pin on the screen.**

7. **Tap Create Spot.**

   Your venue is now complete. Figure 5-1 shows a Gowalla venue.

Figure 5-1:
A venue on
Gowalla.

Yelp

You can't add a Yelp venue from the app, so follow these steps on your computer to set up your venue:

1. **Go to** `http://yelp.com`.

2. **Search for your company's name in the search box.**

3. **Click the Add A Business button at the bottom of your screen.**

4. **Fill in the information about your venue.**

   You provide the following information:

   - *Country*

   - *Business name*

   - *Venue street address*

   - *City, state, and zip code*

   - *Venue phone number*

   - *Website address*

   - *Categories*

     In Categories, you can drill down to as many as three levels depending on the category you choose. If you can't find the right category, choose one that is the closest.

You can check a box that denotes that "This business recently opened or is opening soon" if your business is new. This lets Yelp users know that you didn't just add an existing older venue.

At this point, you're asked to review the location and/or rate it. This may be common sense, but we'd still like to point out that it isn't a good idea to review or rate your own business, as much as you'd like to get things off on the right foot. Consider asking one of your good customers or a friend of your business to do this instead.

5. **Click the Add Business button.**

While you can always go back and edit your information, remember to double-check that all of your information is correct before you submit it.

Facebook Places

When this book went to press, you could create a venue — or *place,* to use Facebook's terminology — using only a smartphone or tablet. To set up your venue on Facebook Places, either open the Facebook app or access the mobile site on your smartphone or tablet by going to `http://touch.facebook.com`. Follow these steps to set up your venue on Facebook Places:

1. **Select Places from the menu (from the drop-down on the mobile touch site or the icon on the Facebook app).**

2. **Click Check In even if your goal is to set up a venue.**

   While this seems counterintuitive, it's the only way to do this to date.

3. **Search for your company's name in the search box.**

4. **Click the Add button.**

5. **Fill in the following information about your place:**

   You're asked to provide the following information:

   • Venue name

   • Description (optional)

6. **Click the Add button.**

   Once you have clicked the Add button — claiming your venue — you'll be able to edit your venue on the Facebook Places website (`http://facebook.com/places`). You can see an example of a Facebook Places post-creation but pre-claim in Figure 5-2.

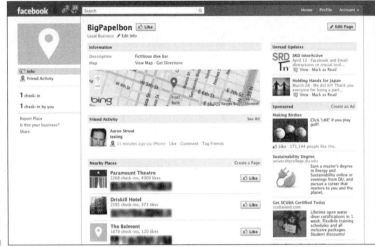

Figure 5-2:
A fictitious
bar cre-
ated on
Facebook
Places post-
creation.

SCVNGR

You can create a venue on SCVNGR using only a smartphone or tablet. To set
up your venue on SCVNGR, open the SCVNGR app on your smartphone or
tablet. Follow these steps to set up your venue on SCVNGR:

1. **Select Places from the menu (from the drop-down on the mobile touch
   site or the icon on the Facebook app).**

2. **Click Check In even if your goal is to set up a venue.**

   While this seems counterintuitive, it's the only way to do create a venue.

3. **Search for your company's name in the search box.**

4. **Click the Add a Place button.**

5. **Fill in the following information about your place:**

   - Venue name
   - Address (this will be pre-filled based on your location but you can
     adjust)
   - City
   - State
   - Postal Code
   - Phone

6. **Click the Add a Place button.**

   You can now edit your venue only after you officially claim it (see Chapter 4).

Editing Your Pages

Whether you set up your venue or someone else did for you to claim, you probably need to edit some of the details or, in some cases, even merge multiple locations. In almost all cases, you need to be the actual owner of the location (not to be confused with the person who leads in check-ins).

On foursquare, venue pages are also edited by participants who foursquare identifies as *superusers,* those who have been power users since the service first launched. As shown in Figure 5-3, a superuser has the ability to edit, merge, or even close venues. If you ever notice a change in your venue information, it might be the handiwork of a superuser. You can rest assured, however, that it's generally assumed that superusers use their administrative powers for good versus tomfoolery. In any case, where you can't fix information on your own, most services have an appeal process that entails e-mailing the service. This can be effective but note that it can often take up to several days to remedy.

If you want to rely on a superuser to keep your page up to date, check out `http://getsatisfaction.com/foursquare`.

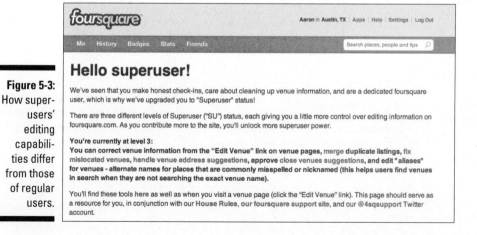

Figure 5-3: How superusers' editing capabilities differ from those of regular users.

(Figure content)

foursquare   Aaron in Austin, TX | Apps | Help | Settings | Log Out

Me   History   Badges   Stats   Friends   Search places, people and tips

Hello superuser!

We've seen that you make honest check-ins, care about cleaning up venue information, and are a dedicated foursquare user, which is why we've upgraded you to "Superuser" status!

There are three different levels of Superuser ("SU") status, each giving you a little more control over editing information on foursquare.com. As you contribute more to the site, you'll unlock more superuser power.

You're currently at level 3:
You can correct venue information from the "Edit Venue" link on venue pages, merge duplicate listings, fix mislocated venues, handle venue address suggestions, approve close venues suggestions, and edit "aliases" for venues - alternate names for places that are commonly misspelled or nicknamed (this helps users find venues in search when they are not searching the exact venue name).

You'll find these tools here as well as when you visit a venue page (click the "Edit Venue" link). This page should serve as a resource for you, in conjunction with our House Rules, our foursquare support site, and our @4sqsupport Twitter account.

While editing your venue, you want to make sure that the basic information about your business is correct, including the venue's phone number, its location on the map and any cross streets, and the category that the service uses to classify your business.

Choosing the right category, adding tips, and uploading photos during the editing and setup process is important. There are a few things that you should pay attention to that can help your customers better interact with your business. One is quite tactical: ensuring that your business is listed under the right category. If you've set up your own venue, there's a good chance you've selected the right category. However, if someone else set up your venue quickly, they might not have been paying too close attention to which category your business belongs in.

It's particularly important to get your category right now that services like foursquare (several other location-based services like Foodspotting and Instagram use foursquare for database purposes) are starting to suggest locations for users who are looking to discover new venues. If you run a hamburger joint and someone filed you under *dive bar,* new users looking for a hamburger joint in your area won't find you in their search results.

Two other aspects of location-based services that you can use to your advantage are tips and photos. While you may be lucky enough to already possess some tips and photos courtesy of customers who checked in before you took ownership of your venue, this shouldn't preclude you from both responding to tips — especially if they're negative — and adding your own photos.

In the case of negative (or even positive) tips, take a conciliatory approach in correcting them or expanding on them. For example, if someone doesn't like your service, you can add a tip like, "We are sorry that some of you have experienced bad service while at our venue. We take these things very seriously and are keeping a closer eye on ways to improve our service. – The Owner."

If your venue is hard to find or near a noticeable landmark, it may not hurt to add a specific tip like, "we are right behind the Jiffy Mart on Main Street" or "our store faces the north side of the park." Regarding photographs, feel free to upload a picture of yourself, your staff, your products, or even your artwork. Remember, the goal here is to engage your customers, so making it a richer experience is a big win.

Integrating multiple social media

Integrating your other social media marketing to your LBS efforts is key to your success. If you're making the effort to set up your business on one of the many LBSs available, you better let your customers know about it via other social networks. We cover integrating your marketing efforts with social networks in greater detail in Chapter 8.

Here are a few general suggestions to get you started:

- ✔ Include links to your website for any of the LBSs that permit you to add one.

- ✔ If you have a Twitter account, add your Twitter handle to the LBSs that allow for one.

  Consider mentioning that you're running an LBS campaign or using a particular tool either in your Twitter profile or in your Twitter background.

- ✔ Is your company on Facebook? Be sure to include a link on your LBS venue page.

  Like Twitter, let your customers know on your Facebook page which LBS you're using.

- ✔ If you maintain a YouTube channel, connect to that as well.

- ✔ Link to any related photo collection on Flickr, Picasa, or Instagram.

  Include a screenshot of your venue in your photo collection and link back to your LBSs of choice.

Integrating into Your CRM System

Now marks the time that customer relation management (CRM) software becomes social. CRM collects direct interaction (sales) with your user base. With social networking, customer data is public. You can now capture both interactions (CRM) and activities (social networking) that users are partaking when they are not interacting with your brand. Social CRM starts in one of four ways:

- ✔ **Private label communities:** These are "invite only" communities where conversations are walled off from the outside world (including search engines). Understanding who is there, what they are talking about, and who they are connecting with is key.

- ✔ **Monitoring social networks:** Using tools like Radian6, Spredfast, and Scout Labs, you can capture and analyze activity across your social and location-based activity.

- ✔ **Facilitating the sharing of common contacts:** If your customers reach you on Twitter or foursquare, you have the ability to acknowledge them across channels.

- ✔ **Community product reviews to facilitate the online sales process:** If you use a service like Bazaarvoice, make sure you know who is creating, rating, and reading your reviews. Be sure you tie this information to user profiles.

Making the data useful and knowing how much data you need to capture is the trick. You can add social information to an existing contact or create a new contact. Here are a few ideas on what information to capture with your CRM:

✔ Grab competitive tweets and manually analyze their sentiment.

✔ Collect mentions of your company, product or services and manually analyze their sentiment.

✔ Collect check-ins to your business.

If your LBS does not have *native integration* (an API that allows for two-way flow of data) to your CRM system, then you should create some manual work-flow. In other words, you need to give the people who have access to your social media monitoring and measurement a way to enrich a customer or prospect's profile with information they find on the Internet. Unfortunately, this may require collecting data manually into a spreadsheet or database and making it available to the necessary parties via the Internet (securely of course).

The idea of tying a CRM to dashboards is a topic that's outside the scope of this book; if you're interested in finding out more, here are some dashboards/CRM systems to look into:

✔ Radian6 is integrated with Salesforce.com via an API (Salesforce.com has acquired Radian6, so the integration between the two companies should eventually get even tighter).

✔ Buzzient has integrations with Oracle CRM on demand, Siebel, Salesforce.com, and SugarCRM. It allows you to "automatically" mine the social web and then create leads and dashboards from your findings.

✔ Community platforms like Jive and Lithium give you the ability to generate and manage content and have conversations on your own site.

Lithium in particular has a brilliant influencer model that allows community managers to figure out who their most valuable participants are. LBSs could be integrated into these systems.

Measuring Your Campaign

While there is little downside to testing location-based marketing, your efforts could be all for naught if you don't take the time to set up a measurement plan. It's a good idea to start thinking about the goals of your campaign at the beginning so that you'll know what you want to measure.

As you're getting started, here are a few things to look for in terms of goals to measure against:

- ✔ **Foot traffic:** Measure this as accurately as possible before, during, and after your campaign.

  As an example, fast food chain McDonald's did a test in 2010 on Foursquare Day, foursquare's annual celebration of its company's existence. The date is April 16 (or the fourth month and day 16, which is 4 squared). According to McDonald's head of social media, Rick Wion, the restaurant's daily check-ins increased by 33 percent and McDonald's spent only $1,000 in gift card rewards.

- ✔ **Share of voice:** This takes a little more work and requires the use of a *listening platform,* or a tool that collects and potentially analyzes conversations across the web from blogs, discussion forums, Twitter, and Facebook.

  Providers include companies such as Radian6, Spredfast, or Converseon. Again, the goal is to see if the conversations about your business on the social web have increased or decreased in relation to your competition. This requires a pre- and post-campaign snapshot to evaluate success.

- ✔ **Increase in sales:** This is obviously one of the best things you could hope for out of your campaign and will be in direct proportion to the offers you decide to present. In some cases, your offer (discussed in greater detail in Chapter 6) will be a *loss leader,* meaning you might lose money on an initial transaction but will make money over time by an increase in transaction size or number of visits.

  This requires some *A/B testing,* which means measuring the sales of a group of customers who aren't offered a special via your LBS versus a group of those that are. This test can tell you if there is a statistically significant increase in sales from one group to the other.

- ✔ **Referrals:** You may need to resort to a qualitative method of measure and track of the number of referrals that come in, on a spreadsheet. To do this, you might incorporate tracking codes in your ads, or you might just ask your new customers who check in how they heard about you.

- ✔ **E-mail marketing:** Some e-mail service providers like Constant Contact are incorporating location through partnerships to build customer loyalty.

- ✔ **Earned media:** Did your campaign get industry publications, bloggers, or even everyday customers to talk about you in a positive way? Tracking this metric also likely requires a spreadsheet. Fortunately, it's easy to track because you will be able to tell whether an article, blog post, or Twitter post includes a reference to your LBS campaign.

We talk more in-depth about measuring your campaign in Chapter 11.

Optimizing Your Campaign

Optimizing your campaign shouldn't be rocket science. It's taking a look at what you're doing and finding ways to make it better.

Often, optimization requires time to elapse so that you have enough data points to effectively measure the components you're tracking. Depending on the volume of your check-ins combined with the nature of what you're trying to measure (many times, qualitative measurement requires less data than quantitative to be statistically significant) it may take a while before you have conclusive data on whether your campaign is succeeding.

One key to optimizing — just like in any well-thought-through marketing campaign — is being careful to isolate what's working and what's not. If you change, or optimize, too many variables too quickly, you can impact the campaign in ways that you can't replicate in the future. So here are a few variables to look at when you're optimizing:

- ✔ **Offers:** The easiest aspect of your campaign to control is your offer. Consider changing the type of offer or adjusting from a coupon discount to a freebie or experience. Which drives the best results? Remember what you're measuring though. If your goal is to get more referrals, you may need to spend more money or time creating an experience versus a discount.

- ✔ **Awareness:** Are you doing the most you can do to promote your location-based campaign? Think about adding table tents, or put stickers or signs on your front door as customers walk in, reminding them to check in. If you don't mention that you're participating in a location-based campaign on your website or Facebook, try doing that to drive greater awareness.

- ✔ **Platform:** Try another location-based service. If you started out on Gowalla, for example, consider testing foursquare, Facebook Places, or Yelp. Compare how two campaigns perform side by side for optimal results.

New entrants in the space like SCVNGR's Level Up and Closely's Social Select enable you to have much more control on the offer (time of day, repeat customers, and referrals).

Looking at the Budget

There isn't a whole lot to say about budget, other than you should definitely have one. If you have a marketing budget, think about how you can carve out a percentage point or two to test with. Maybe you cancel a print or radio ad or forgo a sponsorship or direct mail campaign. Either way, you want to be able to spend enough to make your campaign meaningful without breaking the bank. Of course, if you start to see a meaningful increase in any of the things you're measuring, it's also a good idea to have enough wiggle room to be able to continue your investment.

Defining Where the Responsibilities Lie within the Team

To date, the place where most companies big and small have failed with their location-based efforts has been in the institutionalization of the campaign. That's a fancy way of saying that either the management or social media marketing people forgot to tell the staff or their colleagues about an offer they'd launched, or if they did tell them, it was in passing or via a memo versus taking the time to make sure everyone at the company — at least those who were customer facing — were up to speed on which platform(s) the marketer was using, what your offer(s) entailed, and how to redeem the aforementioned offer.

We'd like to help you avoid that particular pitfall, so here we offer our advice on the subject.

Getting the word out to your organization

Depending on the size of your organization, getting the word out can be as simple as sitting your employees down at lunch with a checklist and walking everyone through all the key details of your campaign. If you work in a larger organization, consider some formal training along with a communications plan that includes multiple touch points. This can include e-mails, posters, an intranet mention, and voice mails, among other tactics.

Making sure your employees are prepared and aware of the rules

First and foremost, you want to make sure that whoever is administering your location-based campaign clearly understands the rules and nuances of the platform you're using. Your LBS administrator should be willing and able to answer any questions regarding the campaign, especially during the first few weeks that it rolls out.

If you own a business that sells things (a restaurant, bar, or antique store, for instance), make sure that you have the offers set up in your point-of-sale (POS) systems. Also be sure to share what the offer is, what it looks like on a variety of different phones, and whether your employees are empowered to make on-the-spot decisions about any trouble that might arise (such as a participant claiming to have checked in but the offer doesn't trigger on his phone).

Print a one-sheet write-up of all the rules with contact information if your employees are unclear about what they're supposed to do. Realistically, they should all be empowered to do the right thing by the customer in the event that there's confusion about the offer.

One additional note — and this is stating the obvious — be sure that you have enough of a supply of whatever you're offering (t-shirts, mugs, lunch slots with the owner, and so on) to run the duration of your campaign. If there's any doubt about whether you'll exceed your supply, consider time-bounding your offer so that you can get a better sense of what your take rate looks like.

If someone has taken the time to check in to your location to take advantage of an offer, you or your staff need to know how to follow up. If you can't figure out what to do, it's a huge momentum killer.

Aligning your technology and internal systems to facilitate an LBS program

If training and communicating with your employees is relatively straightforward, aligning your technology and internal systems to facilitate an LBS program or campaign can be a little trickier. In particular, you may need to get someone from IT involved. Obviously, you'll want to test your program first unless you know that it's part of a bigger corporate initiative that someone else at your organization is testing.

In the former case, test to make sure that a location-based marketing program is right for you, especially if you run a smaller business. If, after a period of time, it seems like the program is working, thinking about importing data into customer relationship management (CRM) systems like Salesforce.com or tying them into your e-mail or web customer contact software like Eloqua makes a lot of sense.

As a larger company, you will likely want to have a series of formal meetings with IT and your legal and PR or corporate communications teams to get everyone on the same page. This will include things like who has admin access to your account (including your own employees), records retention, CRM strategies, and integration into customer service or back-office functions.

If you plan to use a service like shopkick, which is a location-based shopping service, you'll need to install hardware in your store. If you plan to pursue a deeper integration with foursquare, Yelp, or SCVNGR, particularly into your point-of-sale systems, this will of course require the help of your technology teams as well.

Encouraging employee participation

One of the issues that you may bump into is that the people who frequent your venue the most (your employees), are becoming mayors, ambassadors, and so on and thus boxing out other customers from taking advantage of your offers. Be sure to designate certain users as employees or managers on each service. As shown in Figure 5-4, services like foursquare now allow you to delegate certain employees as "staff." Doing this automatically takes those employees out of competition for lead visitor of your venue as well as other customer-only rewards. In order to designate employees as staff, they must be signed up on the service you're using, and you must have claimed your venue.

Figure 5-4: Be sure to designate your staff members as employees.

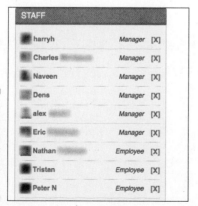

Create challenges, prizes, and awards for employees checking in. Employees in general can be one of your best resources when it comes to tips, creating content, and sharing your venue via their social networks.

Chapter 6

Creating a Relevant Offer

*T*raditional marketing entails making more people aware of your brand and its features and creating an opportunity for customers to purchase your product. You probably focus on casting a wide net, getting as many people in front of your message as possible.

With direct marketing — which location-based marketing is a type of — you can market directly to an individual. Your audience is smaller, typically easier to qualify, and more precisely targeted. The *call to action* — the action you want the recipient to take — in your marketing campaign is something tangible; you may want your potential customer to click a URL, print a coupon, or even make a purchase.

As you can imagine, creating the right offer is one of the most important elements to a successful marketing campaign. In this chapter, we show you how to find your target audience and create a specific offer that they won't be able to refuse!

Determining Your Target Market and Rewarding the Right Customers

Have you ever heard the phrase, "know thy customer"? It's an overused phrase that you've probably said at least once in your career. While the concept of knowing who your customer is may seem painfully obvious, more than a few companies have closed their doors because they failed this simple litmus test.

Location-based marketing isn't any different — in that you need to start any program by understanding who you're trying to appeal to. Knowing your customers and what motivates them will help you better understand what types of offers you should create, along with how much you need to engage them. Figuring this out early and often can help you save countless hours (and dollars) when launching an effective LBS marketing campaign.

Understanding what motivates your customers

Before you can craft your offer, it helps to know who your typical customer is. You can craft an offer using the following info:

- ✔ Is your audience motivated by competitive offers?
- ✔ Can you entice customers by making them feel like they get a special deal when they check in?
- ✔ Will customers check in to your location and play a game to win a small, tangible reward, such as a free cup of coffee?
- ✔ Can you get customers interested in a badge on your company's Facebook Wall?

Because many customers cross-post their check-ins from location-based services to other social networks like Twitter and Facebook, you might consider responding to them on that other network versus just within the LBS. This lets other customers know that you are paying attention and allows people that aren't using location-based services to see that you're running an LBS campaign. You can take a few different approaches, including the following, to determine what offers might be viable to test with your target consumers:

- ✔ **Find out what your competitors are doing.**

    You can look at companies that are similar to yours and see what offers they've tried that have resonated. Look on the venue page of the service itself or do a search on Twitter.

- ✔ **Re-examine your successes.**

    Consider what campaigns and/or offers have worked for you in other channels in the past.

✔ **Ask your customers.**

While this may seem a little straightforward, sometimes asking can be the best way to get to the heart of the matter. If you have a Facebook page or Twitter account, float the idea by some of your customers and see how they respond. If you don't have a Twitter or Facebook account, consider setting up both as they help you in both your location-based and overall social media efforts in tracking and responding to customers on those networks.

Include links to both your Facebook and Twitter accounts on your venue page (if your LBS permits) so that customers can easily navigate to them.

Discovering your loyal customers

If you haven't taken the time to do so, you should do a little due diligence to find out who the regulars are across the major networks that also frequent your physical locations. If you run a small business or chain with just a few locations, this shouldn't be too hard. For bigger retail chains or geographically dispersed companies, this may require the use of some additional tools and resources.

Finding some of your most loyal checkers-in should tell you a little something about what type of LBS customers your business is attracting. It's important to note that these are people who are vying to be top dog at your location even without an offer. Seeking these people out and asking them their opinion on what might make a good offer (as we suggest earlier) will help you get word out about your offer. It will also help you decide which offer to create.

If you have a customer relationship management (CRM) database, consider adding this data over time. If you don't have a CRM, something as simple as a Google document or an Excel spreadsheet might do the trick. Be sure to look on a daily basis if possible, as the person who checks in the most (a mayor on foursquare), can change regularly.

Occasionally, people become so competitive about being the mayor, leader, or duke or duchess of a location that they try to game the system. If you aren't running an offer — which you know we strongly advise against — this won't matter much. But if you are, you don't want someone taking unfair advantage of your offer by cheating. If you notice unusual check-in activity (such as regularly scheduled check-ins around the clock), discretely let them know that you know that they aren't playing fair. This might include commenting on a check-in with a comment such as, "We love that you are checking into our venue every day at the same time. We will be sure to keep an eye out for you next time you are in our store!"

Determining your customers' value

One of the biggest benefits about location-based marketing is that it's quite easy to find more information about the people who are checking into your location(s). For one, many people who use location-based services are also active on other social networks and often cross-post their check-ins to other social networks like Facebook and Twitter. This capability combined with the right offer can provide some deep intelligence on the value (monetary or influence) of your customers.

Follow these steps to find your customers:

1. **Search for your company on the top location-based services.**

   Be sure to check foursquare, Gowalla, SCVNGR, and Facebook Places.

2. **Look for the mayors (in the case of foursquare), top visitors, and people who've left pictures or tips.**

   Figure 6-1 through 6-3 show the Austin-based business, The Donut Hole, on Facebook Places (Figure 6-1), Gowalla (Figure 6-2), and foursquare (Figure 6-3).

   • To find your mayor on *foursquare,* go to http://foursquare.com and search for your venue using the search box at the top of the page. Once you find the venue you're looking for, click it. Then look to the right of the map and you'll find your current mayor.

   • To find your top visitor on *Gowalla,* go to http://gowalla.com and search for a venue using the search box at the top of the page. Once you find the venue you're looking for, click it. Then look underneath the map on the right side of the venue page. Your leaderboard appears in a list below the map.

   • Finding the person who has checked in the most on *Facebook Places* is a little trickier than some of the other services. While you can't currently find the person with the most check-ins, you can find discussions happening at the venue along with any of your friends that have checked in by going to: http://facebook.com/places and searching for a venue using the search box at the top of the page. Once you find the venue you're looking for, click it. Then look in the left-hand navigation on the page for "Discussions" and "Friend Activity."

3. **Click the pictures of the people who check in to your location.**

   If you run a small business, do you recognize them? If they checked in that day, maybe go back through your receipts and take a look at what they bought and how much they spent.

4. **Search for your customer on Google.**

   The more you know about your customers, the better an idea you'll have about what their potential value could be.

5. **Keep notes on anything you find.**

Be careful, though, just as you would in direct marketing. Disclosing to customers how much information you have on them can make them feel a little like they're being cyberstalked.

Figure 6-1:
Facebook
Places is
still in its
early devel-
opment, so
it doesn't
allow you
to see top
visitors.

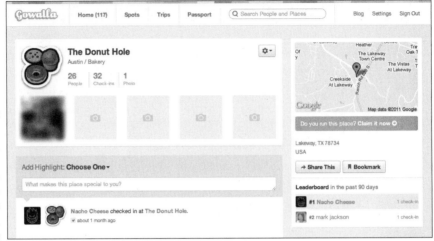

Figure 6-2:
Gowalla's
Leader-
board is
similar to
foursquare's
mayor.

Figure 6-3:
On four-
square, you
can see
the mayor
and the
frequency
of that
person's
check-ins.

Customers who provide tips, recommendations and photos are adding value to your location, so don't forget to pay close attention to them and reward them commensurately.

Rewarding the people who check in

Making your customers aware of the fact that they not only *can* check in but that they *should* check in is critical to location-based marketing. Think through ways to incorporate location-based marketing into all of your customer touch points; for example, you can incorporate your foursquare info on your receipts at checkout; have your salespeople mention your Gowalla URL when answering the phones; and include your Facebook URL in brochures and e-mails, billing statements, and point of purchase displays — and perhaps even direct-response television and radio.

Here are some tactics to consider to reward people for checking in:

- ✔ **Recognize your mayor on foursquare.**

  Offer a free cup of coffee, a special discount, a private lunch or dinner with the owner, or even a special poster with the picture of the mayor.

  It is a mistake to *only* recognize the mayor (or other equivalent across other LBSs). Make sure you offer rewards to others so you don't alienate any potential customers. We discuss tiered rewards in the "Building a tiered rewards system" section later in the chapter.

- ✔ **Consider adding challenges that are specific to your business on a platform that encourages exploration, such as SCVNGR.**

  For example, you can ask customers to find the store manager and introduce themselves for additional prizes or extra points if you use a reward system.

- ✔ **Reward periodic check-ins to encourage ongoing participation.**

  Give away a discount for the first, fifth, and tenth check-ins.

- ✔ **Acknowledge anyone who checks in to your company's physical location(s).**

  It's usually a good idea to wait a few hours before doing this; otherwise, you may come off as creepy. This technique is also best done through social networks like Twitter or Facebook, assuming that your customer decided to cross-post his or her check-in.

Ultimately, create an offer that anyone can take advantage of and then add something extra for the most frequent visitor. This encourages people to come to your business and check in while also creating some competition for the most frequent visitor spot. Figure 6-4 shows a compelling offer that ice cream maker Ben & Jerry's made available during the summer of 2010. Anyone who checked in saved around $2 for a triple scoop of delicious ice cream while the mayor gets a whole extra scoop!

Figure 6-4:
Compelling
foursquare
offer from
Ben &
Jerry's.

Deciding on Offer Types: Paid versus Nonpaid Offers

As we mention earlier in this chapter, you can reward your customers in a number of ways. Some involve items of monetary value, but sometimes, your most valuable offers can come in the form of customer recognition and experience. In the following sections, we discuss paid and nonpaid offers.

Paid offers

Paid offers have some monetary value, whether they are discounts, free t-shirts, free coffee, or gift cards. In many cases, these rewards are great at driving check-ins. Here are some of the major categories of paid offers you can use in your offers:

- ✔ **Free merchandise:** You can offer cups of coffee, dessert, photos, picture frames, t-shirts, posters, or tchotchkes.

- ✔ **Discounts (fixed):** Provide a straight discount for anyone who checks in. Vary the discount by which check-in it is (first, second, and so on) or by the level of engagement.

- ✓ **Discounts (sweepstakes-style):** If you really want to make things exciting, give away a different level of discount as a variable any time someone checks in.

- ✓ **Contests:** Anyone who checks in is entered into a contest for valuable prizes.

Nonpaid offers

Sometimes, the best offers you can make are those of the nonpaid variety. This doesn't mean that you should ignore paid offers, but sometimes simple acknowledgment, a virtual good, or an experience will do the trick. The following lists nonpaid offers that you can incorporate into your LBS marketing campaign:

- ✓ **Acknowledgement:** When customers check in, comment on their check-in or thank them for coming. Remember, don't be overly eager. Sometimes letting some time elapse (at least a few hours) is a good idea.

- ✓ **Customer recognition:** Put a plaque on the wall that lets others know who your mayor, leader, or frequent tip contributor is. Consider posting this information on your website and your Facebook Wall as well.

- ✓ **Virtual goods or badges:** If your customers engage in the gaming aspect of location-based marketing, offer them virtual goods or badges that they can then show off to others.

- ✓ **Experiences:** For your most valuable customers, offer them a tour of your establishment. Or invite a number of your most regular check-ins/contributors to a VIP wine tasting. You might even ask them to become part of a formal or informal advisory board.

To get people excited about sharing their check-ins with their networks, offer the same (or a similar type of discount or offer) to anyone within a customer's network on Twitter or Facebook. To protect yourself, you can bind the offer or discount by location or time frame.

Understanding the Components of Offers

Offers are the lifeblood of any successful LBS marketing campaign. Understanding how they work and what types of behaviors they drive is critical to engaging with your customers. This section discusses some of the nuances of creating an offer to drive different types of engagement.

Rewarding the influencer

Earlier in the chapter, we talk about the ability to learn more about your customers by diving a little deeper by Googling them or looking up their profile on LinkedIn. This is good when you're trying to determine whether a customer is an *influencer* (someone who has clout in the online world). However, this can be a double-edged sword if customers know that you're offering specials to your influencers.

One way around appearing to favor your influencers is to focus on more experiential-types of rewards, such as VIP get-togethers and advisory board invites. Conversely, if influencers know that your business provides higher-level rewards for people with clout, you may get a disproportionate number of check-ins from people with influence. This is not a bad thing.

Creating a check-in special for everyone

Sometimes, when you're just getting started with your location-based marketing program, providing a uniform offer for anyone who checks in can be the easiest to administer. Think of it as analogous to a happy hour special. In fact, this offer might look similar to one that you would offer to a new customer, something like free service for a month or a free drink. If you sell tickets, you might offer 50 percent off a second ticket of equal value.

Building a tiered rewards system

Having a tiered rewards system can often ensure that you're not only rewarding your most valuable customers but also providing incentives for people to keep checking in. If you've ever been to a fair or carnival, you might have observed that the people who run the games have this practice down to a science. You'll notice that almost everybody wins, but the first prize you win is usually worth less than the value of what you pay to play. It's not until you've invested in the game multiple times that you win the huge stuffed lion or the really cool Lady Gaga mirror.

You may also want to consider a tiered rewards system depending on the way your customer has chosen to interact with you. For instance, a mayorship or being top of the Leaderboard might merit the highest reward because it demonstrates the highest level of loyalty. Check-ins may merit a different reward (with perhaps the first gaining a more meaningful reward), and added tips and photos yet another reward.

Recent offerings from companies like SCVNGR with the Level Up platform and Closely's Social Select enable you to provide different offers to different customers based on loyalty, time of day, and other variables. Specifically

✔ **Level Up:** This service provided by SCVNGR is geared at competing with group couponing services like Groupon and LivingSocial. The service offers three deals a day and each deal is unlocked by exploring each of the three businesses offering the deal.

✔ **Social Select:** You can target specific customers so only the customers you invite to explore are eligible. However, once your target customers "unlock" a deal, they can share with their networks.

Unlocking better offers

Creating a tiered offer is important if you want to keep people coming back again and again. (See the preceding section for more info on tiered offers.) One way to do this is to explicitly let customers know that the more they check in, the better the offers get. A more clever way to do this is to offer up surprise rewards after an initial check-in.

For example, Mazda announced a foursquare offer where customers could check in to a location to get additional information about where they needed to check in next. Eventually, participants who made it far enough into the check-in schedule were eligible to win a Mazda2. This type of approach makes playing the game (or checking off the requisite activities) almost as fun as thinking about winning the big prize.

Surprising people with badges and games

In the "Nonpaid offers" section earlier in this chapter, we mention the importance of a *badge* (an icon that is earned for checking in at a particular location or a series of locations). Currently, several of the LBSs offer badges. foursquare has an entire section of its website dedicated to the types of badges that participants can earn. These badges range from the obvious Newbie (first time ever checking in on foursquare) or Adventurer (checked into ten different locations), to the more esoteric Crunked (four plus stops in one night) or Player Please (checked in with three members of the opposite sex) badges.

Figure 6-5 shows a partial list of some of the badges awarded by foursquare.

Check out a full list of foursquare badges at www.4squarebadges.com/ foursquare-badge-list.

Figure 6-5:
A sample
list of
badges of
popular LBS
platform
foursquare.

For example, Milwaukee-area burger joint AJ Bombers (http://www.ajbombers.com or @ajbombers) used a grassroots effort to get people into restaurants. They held a "swarm party." The *swarm* badge is given when 50 people check in to a single location. They got 161 people to check in.

Answering "How Big Do I Need to Go?" with a Test-and-Learn Strategy

Depending on the size of your industry and size of your business, some offers will work better than others. The test-and-learn strategy is the best way to innovate. You use your initial campaign to set benchmarks, and design subsequent campaigns to beat those benchmarks based on what you learned about your audience during the last campaign.

The easiest piece to test is the offer, but you can test other audience variables as well, such as various offers versus different goals. For instance, using acknowledgement and recognition to build loyalty might be one area to test. Trying varying levels of discounts, giveaways, games, and even experiences might be the way to go for customer acquisition or retention.

Ingenuity goes a long way when it comes to customer adoption and earned media.

Learning from others who have tested the waters

For better or worse, only a few dozen Fortune 500 companies have tested the waters in the world of location-based marketing. We assume that there will be many more after this book is published, but here are a few case studies from well-recognized brands that are worth looking into:

✔ **Murphy USA:** It tapped into Whrrl (now a part of Groupon) to provide discounts and free gas to loyal customers.

    http://www.clickz.com/
    clickz/news/1721820/
    murphys-usa-creates-
    loyalty-program-with-
    location-based-service-
    whrrl

✔ **New Jersey Nets:** Randomly gave away tickets to Gowalla members who checked into specific locations.

    http://www.nba.com/
    nets/news/Gowalla_
    Release_100407.html

✔ **Gap:** Offered 10,000 pairs of jeans to the first 10 check-ins in Gap stores across the country.

    http://www.fastcompany.
    com/1700976/did-gaps-
    free-jeans-facebook-deal-
    disappoint-customers

✔ **Robert Mondavi Wineries and Franciscan Estates:** Partnered with SCVNGR to offer rewards for playing games at their venues.

    http://mashable.
    com/2010/11/11/scvngr-
    napa-valley-rewards

Placing multiple offers into the marketplace

You need to be careful not to put too good of an offer out into the market. Don't bank on the law of averages to protect you from spending hundreds of millions (or billions) of dollars on promotional giveaways.

To avoid this, test multiple offers in the marketplace at the same time. In doing so, you can avoid confusion by segmenting offers by the following:

✔ **Geography:** Push out different tests in different cities.

✔ **Time and date:** Try different offers at different times of the day or different days of the week.

✔ **Multilevel offers:** Allow customers to unlock better offers the more they engage.

✔ **Customer's choice:** Provide two or three items of similar value and let the customer pick.

✔ **Random:** Offer several items of similar value and randomly distribute them. Take notes on customers' reactions.

Evaluating the ROI of an offer

At the end of the day, the most important thing about any marketing campaign is that you get a return on your investment (ROI) — even if it's just your time. One of the things that is tricky in the world of social media is that while all things are measurable, some of the benefits that social media offer — and thus location-based marketing — can be a little less tangible than that of say an e-mail or search marketing campaign.

Less-tangible, longer-term benefits include things like share of conversation, lifetime value, customer loyalty (as measured by indicators like Net Promoter Score), and customer engagement. We get into ways to measure all of these things in Part III in this book.

For things that you can measure, including increase in traffic, increase in reach and frequency of your message, increase in sales and share of wallet, any one of them can be explicitly linked to location-based marketing. However, it does require the discipline of getting back to marketing 101 principles. This means keeping close track of all the variables of the campaign and being careful to keep them as limited as possible. For instance,

✔ **Do pre- and post- testing.**

If you're looking to drive foot traffic, measure how much foot traffic comes into your store before you make an offer on an LBS and then after.

✔ **A/B test with locations, offers, or time periods.**

A/B testing involves testing one element of a campaign (for instance, an offer) versus another while keeping all other elements the same. For example, in an e-mail campaign, you might randomly split a list of 10,000 people in half and offer one set a 20 percent discount and the other a free pen. This helps you determine which elements of your campaign are the most effective.

For location-based marketing, create a test where you offer a free item in one location or market and then a 20 percent discount in another. (The free item is your A, and the 20 percent discount is your B.) If you use an offer management tool like Geotoko, performing an A/B test across venues, or platforms is immeasurably easier.

✔ **Watch the market.**

Keep an eye on market factors, holidays, and other external factors that can have an impact.

 Focus on offers that might be larger or less scalable than normal to get some initial traction with your location-based marketing program. Binding your offers by time period or with the age-old "while supplies last" can help protect you from going bankrupt.

Chapter 7

Using Location-Based Marketing to Enhance a Loyalty Program

*B*efore you have a customer, you have prospects. Prospects become customers. Customers come in different flavors, from casual to devoted. And sometimes customers leave for greener pastures. Many companies expend incredible amounts of resources and energy to get people to become customers — and then to *stay* customers. They buy ads on TV and radio, keywords on Google, put coupons in blue envelopes, and sometimes dress up in moose suits and attempt to flag down people. The acquisition game is costly, so once you get customers, it makes sense to do your very best to keep them happy.

The airlines have point-based loyalty programs that reward customers for their business. Rental car companies, hotels, credit card companies, and even grocery stores have built similar loyalty programs to reward people who use their services.

You can implement the same idea with your location-based marketing. Combine a loyalty program to reward your existing customers with location-based services that offer additional rewards. In this chapter, we show you how to use a location-based service to keep the customers you already have.

If you're serious about building a loyalty program, be sure to include four-square, which encourages specials designed to entice your existing customers into coming back for more. While you may get new people into your store, that's considered a bonus.

Transforming Loyalty into Social Loyalty

Loyalty programs are built to reward people who use your products and services. Think of these loyalty offers like a Nintendo game. Like Super Mario Brothers, they involve points and levels. Like The Legend of Zelda, the more a customer does, the more time he spends interacting with your business, the more rewards and powers he can unlock and the more powerful he becomes. Airlines work on a similar principle; you need a gold or better status to get the free upgrade to first class. Programs work this way:

1. Convince customers to sign up for your program.

2. Customers purchase your products or services to earn points.

3. Customers buy more products or services to earn more points.

4. Customers redeem their points for an upscale product or service that's otherwise unattainable.

    With a loyalty program, you generate good feelings toward your brand and get the people who are using your brand products to ultimately buy more products more frequently.

So how do you incorporate a social media aspect into a loyalty program? You can incorporate your LBS accounts to give users chances to unlock specials and even earn additional points or unlock offers that are specific to each customer.

When you incorporate location-based solutions into your loyalty program and promote that fact, you give people a reason to sign up for a location-based service. In the following sections, we explore how you can make your loyalty programs easy to sign up for, thus getting people who might not normally use a location-based service to become regular users.

Searching social data

The location aspect of social media is a major advancement in loyalty. The convergence of social activity streams can get you closer to the Holy Grail of marketing — knowing as much about a customer as possible so that you can put the most meaningful offer in front of her. If you know where (location), and what a customer is buying, you can create an offer specifically designed for that customer. You have a good chance of building loyalty and therefore retain that customer.

Location gives you some very important data points, including the following, that can help you get to know your customers:

- ✔ **Hometown:** Unless a person is checking in to an airport, you can use check-ins to figure out where that person lives. The likelihood is that a customer can change her behavior if the place is close by because it's easy.

- ✔ **Place loyalty:** This data point tells you whether a person is loyal to a place because of its location or that person goes out of his way to get a favorite brand.

- ✔ **Brand loyalty:** Brand loyalists go out of their way to use a brand wherever they are whenever they have a use for that brand. For the most loyal people, no other brand will do. For example: Some people are so loyal to Pepsi that they will never drink Coke. This goes the same for places. For some people, Starbucks is no substitute for Dunkin Donuts.

- ✔ **Frequency:** Sometimes the proximity of an offer to the places that a person visits the most matters.

- ✔ **Travel habits:** If you see a customer checking in to a lot of airports, you know that he is a frequent traveler. You need to give him a reason to be loyal to your brand, even if he has to go out of his way.

When you have this information, you have all the components of a good offer:

- ✔ **Portray the value of your product.**

    Say, maybe 10 percent off a cup of coffee because you know your customer drinks coffee at your store.

- ✔ **Respect the customer.**

    If your customer comes into your coffee store every business day, offer a free cup of coffee once a month.

- ✔ **Give the customer a reason to respond.**

    You know your customer prefers coffee over tea, so give him a coffee offer.

- ✔ **Fit in what the customer is already doing.**

    Make your offer during a weekday because you know he's there every morning for his daily cup.

Making check-ins passive

Loyalty programs have the potential to make check-ins a lot easier by linking your business's loyalty program to a customer's LBS account (for example, foursquare). Then, you can push any reward offers to that customer.

Say, a customer signs up for your loyalty program. When she signs up, she gives you permission to send LBS offers to her phone when she enters your store. You catch your customer — with the perfect offer because you know what she likes — at the right time and place where she can take advantage of it. The fact that she entered your store checks her in. She doesn't have to do anything to get the offer — that's a passive check-in. You can build this functionality into your API, as shown in Figure 7-1. It may not be obvious to you here, but this one is clean and beautiful, which encourages use by developers.

Figure 7-1: foursquare clearly understands that an API needs to be simple, reliable, and well documented.

Tasti D-Lite: The pioneers of social loyalty

Tasti D-Lite offers frozen desserts and treats to an intensely loyal following through 50 franchises around the U.S. and abroad. In addition to traditional credit and gift card transactions, Tasti D-Lite's socially friendly point-of-sale system was recently nominated for QSR's Applied Technology Award for its integrative approach to loyalty programs.

BJ Emerson, VP Technology, points out that franchisees seek to "reward customers with loyalty points for sharing experiences related to the brand." Thus, TreatCard (loyalty card) holders earn points on purchases. By registering

a card online at MyTasti.com, a customer can link a Tasti D-Lite account to accounts on Twitter, Facebook, and foursquare (see the following figure). In doing so, they can easily share their Tasti experiences with friends and followers while earning extra rewards toward future purchases.

With a swipe of a TreatCard at the cash register, customers can automatically check in on foursquare while getting their Tasti fix. At the time of publishing, approximately 25 percent of customers were linking their TastiRewards accounts to at least one social network, with an average of over 90 friends or followers in each. Tasti D-Lite also plans to eventually include unique coupon codes traceable back to the original check in. For instance, a customer will be able to swipe his card at Tasti to automatically check in on foursquare while simultaneously pushing a coupon to other social networks. If 10 friends or followers subsequently redeem the coupon, that's 10 extra loyalty points as a result of the original check-in — effectively taking word-of-mouth marketing to an entirely new level.

The foursquare app helps Tasti D-Lite employ location-based campaigns while providing opportunities to highlight specials to foursquare users who check-in, so users get great discounts via foursquare check-ins that other people aren't privy to. It's authentic and fun. The flip side is Tasti D-Lite gaining insights into consumer behavior.

BJ emphasizes a completely new metric that he can now measure. He says that "check-ins represent feet in the door" as opposed to clicks, impressions, and other common online measurements.

This new metric includes total check-ins at a given location, deals redeemed from specials nearby, where people come from, messages pushed to Facebook and Twitter from within the location, and so on. These new data points offer a wealth of information for Tasti D-Lite to tap into and analyze. For instance, click-through rates of specials nearby are near 40 percent with a check-in rate of over 7 percent — which translates into this new "feet in the door" metric.

The value to Tasti D-Lite, according to BJ, is "greater engagement with customers. New customers are acquired through nearby specials. Existing customer loyalty is encouraged through the TastiRewards/foursquare integration."

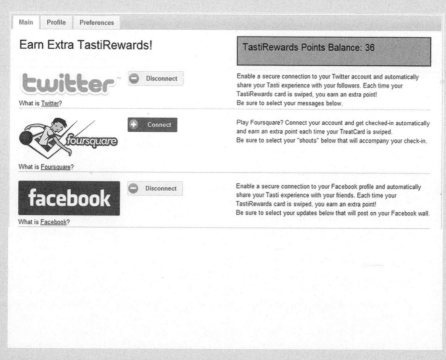

Collecting Customer Information for Your Loyalty Program

Check-in data allows you to get a very good picture of where people go — or at least where they're checking in. That information is great, but you can get so much more data when you combine check-ins with a loyalty program.

When you offer a loyalty program, people are often willing to give more information. The answers to these questions allow you to put an offer in the hands of the customer that is highly relevant.

- ✔ Where do you live?
- ✔ Are you a traveler?
- ✔ What places do you frequent?
- ✔ What places do you like to visit?
- ✔ How often do you visit places?
- ✔ Are you loyal to a place or to a brand?
- ✔ Are you loyal to a brand when it is near a competitor?
- ✔ How often do you visit competitive brands?

You want data on the everyday behavior of your customers and prospects. The more data you have about them, the more you know about their preferences.

Aligning location with stream of consciousness and purchase behavior

Location and place are pieces of data that fuel activity streams. An *activity stream* is a list of activities performed by a user, usually listed in order of recency. Activity streams typically serve a single purpose and provide structure around that purpose. Here are some examples of activity streams and platforms that enable them:

- ✔ **Taking pictures:** Platforms like Flickr (www.flickr.com), Facebook (www.facebook.com), and Instagram (instagr.am) do a great job of capturing life in photos. They also offer you a way to show the inside of your business, pictures of your staff, and general goings-on in your business.

✔ **Streams of consciousness:** Platforms like Twitter (www.twitter.com) and Facebook are great at capturing whatever is at top of mind. You get access to things like a person's friends, the brands they talk about, the ones they like and do not like, product ideas, interests, and professional ideas.

✔ **Product exploration:** An application called Stickybits (www.sticky bits.com) tracks a user scanning product barcodes and the content the user creates for those bar codes. You can see what products people are passionate enough to check in to and what they think about the product.

✔ **Checking into books, movies, and TV shoes:** GetGlue (www.getglue.com) and Miso (sometimes called Go Miso because it's gomiso.com) keep track of the books that someone has read. Knowing the kinds of books a person reads, TV shows they watch, and games they play tell you a lot about their media preferences and allow you to target people based on those preferences. See Figure 7-2 for a look at GetGlue.

✔ **Drinking beer:** Apps like Untappd (www.untappd.com) track what beer someone is drinking and where he's enjoying the beer. Untappd is even integrated with foursquare so there's just one check-in for the location and the beer, not two separate ones.

✔ **Eating:** The Foodspotting (www.foodspotting.com) app lets someone take pictures of food at places they eat and share them. It helps you get user-generated exposure. Knowing a person's food choices and where they are eating gives you a sense of not only where they eat and what they eat (vegan, carnivore, omnivore) but whether they have a culinary sense of adventure.

Figure 7-2:
GetGlue lets you check in to shows, music, books, movies, games, thoughts, and wine.

- ✔ **Shopping carts:** Using applications powered by Modiv (`www.modiv media.com`) and Aislebuyer (`http://aislebuyer.com`) let customers in your store scan barcodes with their phones, thereby building a shopping cart, and then buy the items without ever going near a cash register.

- ✔ **Purchases:** Apps like Blippy (`www.blippy.com`) and Swipely (`www.swipely.com`) ask for access to e-commerce accounts like Amazon, iTunes, and eBay. It scans e-mail for receipts and, if the user allows, records the transactions on credit cards. This gives you a sense of the size of a person's wallet, their purchase preferences, and frequency outside of your business.

These applications represent advanced uses of location-based marketing. Following from check-in to the purchase is highly desirable, but still fairly difficult.

Most importantly, access to stream of consciousness and location data gives you the data to create a profile based on personal preferences, profession, and competitive and loyal behavior.

Looking at Loyalty Program and Structured Data

Activity streams give you structured data, which you can easily store in a database, query (find), and aggregate (summarize) in your reports. A database is designed to bring structure to your data and build relationships between real world happenings so that software and people in various roles from marketers to analysts can make sense of it later. Databases are made up of entities that are basically anything you want to store at the highest level. Customer, place, and product are examples of entities. They are made up of attributes (also known as fields) like business name, address, city, state, zip code, and phone number.

Good databases usually have rules that cleanse data into one standard format. For example, states: If you leave people to their own devices, you will get many different versions of the state of Massachusetts. People will type: Mass, Massachusetts, ma, MA, Ma. In a database, it's stored in the state field as MA. This makes querying (finding) every place in Massachusetts a lot easier.

The odds are you already have a database. The trick is to add loyalty data to it to extract meaningful insight. You can pull out and sort any fields you want to look at a subset of data. With loyalty data you can get a pretty good idea of who your customers are. Loyalty is made up of entities like customer, purchase, product, place, points, and rewards. Your business is (hopefully) already capturing a fair amount of this data and needs only add a way to give points and rewards.

In a non-social loyalty program, you are only getting one piece of the puzzle because you're limited to the data that you collect at your business. Adding social data from check-ins and tweets can add a lot to the customer entity.

In structured data, your options are limited — all data must fit into a field — but the data is easier to analyze. In other words, when someone checks in to your place on foursquare, there's only one record of that particular place so that when you look at all of the people that check into your place, you don't need to write special code to extract data from multiple locations. It makes activity streams easier to analyze and combine with other activity streams.

Take Twitter for example. Imagine if you have access to a customer or prospect's Twitter and LBS accounts. You can discover the following information:

- ✓ Place of business
- ✓ Brands they interact with
- ✓ Brands they like and dislike
- ✓ Who they influence
- ✓ Who influences them
- ✓ Professional opinions
- ✓ Personal passions and interests
- ✓ Their ideas

You could use all of this information to build a communication strategy. Segment your customers by common elements (maybe by brand) and group them together so that you can build messages that resonate with people.

Mining conversations allows you to build a very detailed profile of your customers based on subject, sentiment, and frequency. In the following sections, we discuss the kind of data that you can find out about your customers through a loyalty program: conversations, loyalty (whether it's place or brand), and purchases. You can call it the holy triad of marketing.

Figure 7-3 shows a game board that gives you how the data you get is a progression. Start with stream of consciousness data. Find out things like a person's profession, their interests, ideas, and who they find important. Couple that with their location on the right side of the board; you get interesting things, such as brand loyalty, place loyalty, whether they are a traveler. If you can add their purchase behavior (bottom of the board), you get to unlock things like your share of their wallet and the size of their wallet. Getting all of this data lets you build really smart, specialized, targeted offers.

It's a game board because it goes back to collection of data to see how customers react to offers, you can learn more about their preferences, and change the way you interact with them. It's a never ending cycle and you do not necessarily need all of the data to get started. Any of the three activity streams give you a good idea of how a person behaves.

Figure 7-3:
The Allen & Gerritsen and CauseShift Loyalty in 4-D game board shows how social, location, purchase, and offers create the ultimate test-and-learn environment.

Courtesy of Allen & Gerritsen

Streams of consciousness data

You can group people based on the subjects of their conversations, the way they feel about the topic, and how often they participate in the conversation.

Set up a table that analyzes conversations. You can then prioritize messages based on the highest frequency. You can segment the data by conversation types that people participate in and you can decide whether you want to participate in the kinds of conversations that your prospects like.

Finding frequency, brand, and place loyalty

Looking strictly at place data, you can learn where a person goes, which is great because it tells you how often a person frequents a certain place, and that tells you how often that place is contextually relevant to that person.

Presumably, when consumers go to a place of business, they buy things. Making offers to people in that place may get them to buy more things or make purchases that they weren't expecting to make.

Purchase data

The most elusive data is what a customer purchased, particularly purchases for more than one place, or for places you don't own. Most point of sale systems are capturing items purchased along with a credit card number and storing them in an antiquated database. Loyalty programs can give you a clear picture of what a person purchased, but they only give you the items that have been purchased at your company.

Implementing a Loyalty Program

Technology makes it possible to target a group of willing audience members and to turn them into powerful advocates. In the following sections, we take a look at two ways you can start using a loyalty program.

Many people may feel leery about giving up as much private information as you're asking them for with a loyalty program. With encryption, programs take the info your customer inputs into a service and makes it unreadable to the average person. You can then translate the data back into meaningful data by using an encryption key. You can provide this security measure to reassure customers that their data isn't being misused and is being kept secure.

Encryption takes a lot of technical know-how. If you don't feel up to the task, make sure you hire someone you explicitly trust. Setting up an encryption code gives that person access to very privileged information.

Creating online punch cards

Punch cards are what loyalty programs used to be about. You probably have used *punch cards* before — those cards that you get punched (or stamped) a certain number of times and then you get a free product.

Punch cards are a relatively easy way to do loyalty, but they have certain disadvantages. For instance, punch cards are anonymous. You don't actually know anything about the customer because no personal information is attached to the card. You most likely do not know how many times a customer has redeemed a loyalty card. Anyone can pick up a card and use it. You know someone used a card, and that's it.

Punchd is an iPhone and Android app, shown in Figure 7-4, that lets you use the idea of a punch card. You add the Punchd capability to your register, and when a customer makes a purchase, she can scan her phone. Her punch is recorded, and when she collects the designated number of punches she's rewarded.

Figure 7-4: Punchd offers a simple way to make punch cards more useful.

Creating applications

The processing power on an iPhone and Android phone is staggering. You can use the technology built into today's smartphones to make using a loyalty program easy and more convenient — no having to carry around a card or ID number. Customers can scan their phones right at the register to cash in on their points. Soon, technology like near field communication (NFC) will make checking in via a loyalty program even easier by allowing a user to tap a phone at the register to check in or record a purchase. This convenience is a great way to reward your loyal customers.

For example, Starbucks offers a couple apps. myStarbucks allows a customer to find a location, create and share a drink, and find the nearest store. Mobile Card allows a customer to enter a loyalty card number and scan the app at the register to pay for purchases. The app shows the card balance and recharges the card. Between January and March 2011, three million people paid for their coffee with Mobile Card.

The Cardstar app for iPhone and Android has digitized loyalty by allowing a customer to store the bar codes from your shopping loyalty programs on a phone (see Figure 7-5). Recent integration with Groupon also allows Cardstar users to see surrounding Groupon Deals. Marketers should push for the same with their foursquare specials. Eliminating additional steps (like going into a separate app to see if there are specials) will make location-based marketing that much easier to add to a user's daily dealings.

Figure 7-5:
Cardstar allows someone to store bar codes and scan them at the register.

Part III
Integrating Location into Other Channels

The 5th Wave   By Rich Tennant

"Before the Internet, we were only bustin' chops locally. But now, with Facebook Places, we're bustin' chops all over the world."

In this part . . .

Part III shows you how to integrate your campaign into other social networks like Twitter and Facebook, and how to add a location aspect in your other marketing.

In this part, you discover more about

- The best way to integrate LBS into places like Twitter and Facebook
- How to think about location beyond the check-in
- Ways to help your customers find you on places like Bing and Yahoo!

Chapter 8

Integrating Location-Based Marketing with Other Marketing Campaigns

---

In This Chapter

▶ Understanding the difference between paid, earned, and owned media

▶ Discovering how paid, earned, and owned media can work together

▶ Taking full advantage of social networks like Facebook and Twitter

▶ Looking at how users access location-based services

---

*I*n this chapter, we show you how to most effectively spread the word about your campaign with the *holy trinity* of media — paid, earned, and owned. These include advertising (paid), your website, or places like Facebook, Twitter, and YouTube, along with your physical properties (owned) and public relations, as well as conversations about you on the social web (earned).

Understanding the Differences between Different Media

Understanding the differences between different media types and how the three work best together is key when it comes to building a good location-based marketing campaign.

✔ **Paid:** Paying to leverage the power of a channel to drive eyeballs to your content or call to action. You use it to cast a wide net and drive qualified eyeballs to a property. This is the most scalable and predictable of the three media types. It also has the longest track record of the three, making it the best understood. Click-through rates are typically low and are continuously declining as people lose trust in big media.

 ✔ **Owned:** A channel that is controlled by a person or brand. The key is that other platforms, brands, or people cannot change the experience without your permission. You create content that builds relationships and gives customers and prospects more reasons to interact with your brand. You maintain control, you can do whatever you want whenever you want to; no one can yank the rug out from under you. You have no guarantees that anyone will see your owned media.

 ✔ **Earned:** The customer as a channel. This levels the playing field between people and brands. There is no transparency and you have ability to reach anyone. But you have no control and may come across some negativity.

Figure 8-1 shows a chart from marketer Allen & Gerritsen spelling out definitions, roles, examples, strengths, and challenges of each type of media.

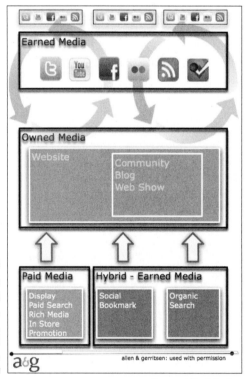

Figure 8-1:
A matrix on paid, earned, and owned media.

Courtesy of Allen & Gerritsen

Paid, earned, and owned media work best in conjunction with one another. Paid media may not be as popular as it once was, but earned and owned media have increased in popularity.

Paid Media

Paid media is something that takes very little effort on your part. You hand over your money, and your ad gets placed. Your money goes toward leveraging a certain channel. Examples include

- Display ads on a web portal like Yahoo! or news site like TheNewYorkTimes.com.

- Paid search results on Google or Bing like the ones for coffee shops in Figure 8-2.

- Sponsorships at large sporting events or conferences.

- Radio ads.

- Print circulars in the Sunday paper.

- Outdoor ads.

- Mobile advertising, Facebook ads, and sponsored tweets.

Before you hand over your money, keep these things in mind:

- **Paid media is diminishing in popularity.**

  Though it still earns a big share of marketing dollars, it's becoming increasingly less relevant. People generally get recommendations from people they trust, rather than random advertising.

Figure 8-2:
Paid search
results
for coffee
shops on
search
engine,
Bing.

Paid search ads

✓ **Paid media has a lot of competition for people's attention.**

There are billions of pieces of content — videos, pictures, updates, podcasts, blogs — on the thousands of social networking sites.

If you run a small business and want to consider affordable paid activities to drive customers to your location-based marketing campaign, here are a few to think about budgeting for:

✓ **Place ads in local or national newspapers (print or online) depending on your size.**

Figure 8-3 shows how Buffalo Wild Wings incorporates SCVNGR into its campaign advertising.

✓ **Buy paid keyword buys with Google or Bing.**

Paid keyword campaigns is the buying of search terms that fit your business through a bid process. The highest bidder on a certain keyword like "computers" gets an ad displayed at the top or side of the results page. If you want more information on how paid search works, the major search engines like Google and Bing provide tutorials and FAQs on their sites (see for example, `http://adwords.google.com`).

✓ **Offer extra inventory to your local cable or radio station.**

Sometimes, in-kind exchanges (food for airtime, for instance) can work, especially for less desirable time slots like the late-night shift.

✓ **Rent an outdoor billboard.**

If your business is big enough, a billboard might be a reasonable way to let your local market know that you're participating in a location-based marketing campaign. We outline how the New Jersey Nets incorporated billboards into its location-based marketing in the nearby sidebar. You probably don't have the budget of the Nets, but if you shop around, you can find many local billboards that are much more reasonable.

Figure 8-3: BW3 incorporates SCVNGR into its paid advertising.

Courtesy of Buffalo Wild Wings®

How the New Jersey Nets used a billboard to drive a Gowalla campaign

If you live in New York City, in April 2010 you may have noticed a ten-story building at 38th Street and 8th Avenue painted with likenesses of Russian billionaire Mikhail Prokhorov and rap star Jay-Z, the new owners of the NBA's New Jersey Nets. At the very bottom of that 10-story billboard in midtown Manhattan was a unique call to action that few people had ever seen before. In addition to including a phone number and the team's Twitter and Facebook account information, the Nets asked that passersby "Check In with Gowalla to Get a Special Item."

While there were many components to this campaign, including a ticket giveaway and blog posts by both the Nets and Gowalla, it was this paid outdoor signage in this high-traffic area of New York (right near Penn Station) that kicked things off for the Nets.

The goal of the campaign was to introduce a new demographic target to Nets basketball while sparking interest in what was the worst team in the NBA that year. To do so, users were encouraged, just like the billboard said, to check in to Gowalla within a 75-mile perimeter of the Izod Center (the Nets home court). For checking in, fans had a chance to win 250 pairs of Nets tickets. Of the tickets given away, 15.2 percent were redeemed. The Nets, Gowalla, and the agency that put this together, VaynerMedia, viewed this as a success. More importantly, it drove a lot of earned media coverage, which was a secondary goal of the campaign.

Earned Media

Unlike paid media, earned media is a little trickier concept to grasp. With *earned media,* customers spread the word about your company, brand, or campaign — you essentially earn their trust enough to help you with marketing. This includes all those phrases you've heard over the years, including *word of mouth, buzz,* and *viral.* It also includes good old-fashioned public relations (press releases, e-mails, and phone calls).

Earned media is far from free and when done properly requires a lot of your time and elbow grease. The upside is that unlike paid media that requires constant care and feeding (not to mention money), earned media is more like an annuity. Even if your earned media efforts are bound by time and *reach* (number of people who actually read or see your message), check-ins (which are earned media) are increasingly coming up in search results on Google and Bing. If someone searches for your business or does a local search for your category, there's a decent chance that one of your customers' check-ins could come up on the top results page.

In addition to being search-friendly, location-based marketing can also help generate other earned media with traditional media, bloggers, and your customers. The New Jersey Nets received coverage in the form of hundreds of articles and blog posts. (Just do a Google search on *Gowalla NJ Nets.*) In addition, tweets included numerous ecstatic updates from Gowalla users who checked in and won virtual tickets to be traded for tickets to the game. (See Figure 8-4.)

Figure 8-4:
Tweets
during the
NJ Nets
Gowalla
ticket
giveaway
campaign in
2010.

One avenue to good earned media is having the right offer. Create an experience, such as meet the chef, owner, designer, or head of product development. Host a wine tasting or ice cream sundae party. Not only will you get people talking about it, but the people who attend will post pictures, Facebook status updates, tweets, and maybe even a blog post. With enough conversation about a particular topic, the traditional press — many of whom are now on Twitter and Facebook — may start to take notice.

Here are a few suggestions on things that you can do to drive more earned media:

- **Create a council or ambassador program.**

  Tap some of your best customers and get them together quarterly in person or via phone to ask them what they think of your program, offer, or platform.

- **Create a special day at your venue(s).**

  Invite the current top-checker-inner to give a little talk. Offer free coffee, cookies, sliders, cocktails, or whatever you can afford. Invite the local press to the event; you can usually find their contact information on their web pages.

- **Start with a game.**

  Even if you decide to go with Yelp, Gowalla, Facebook Places, or foursquare as your platforms, start with a scavenger hunt on SCVNGR. Make it coincide with a big event in your town or city like a Victorian fair, a holiday celebration, or the local carnival coming to town. Give away prizes — they don't have to be fancy — to the top 20 teams or individuals.

- **Make sure that your paid and earned campaigns coordinate so that you can get the maximum bang for your buck.**

  If you do Facebook ads or take out a full-page ad in your local paper, point readers to a specific activity or series of activities.

Look at what some of the businesses in your area have done and what has resonated with customers by doing a few Google or Twitter searches. (Use http://search.twitter.com to search Twitter.) foursquare has a number of local business programs at http://foursquare.com/business.

One of the biggest mistakes you can make is not preparing for what happens after you've initiated a campaign. For example, TGI Friday's offered a free hamburger to their first 500,000 Facebook fans, but did not think far enough ahead on how to engage fans once they signed up. You can waste a lot of money and time by not thinking through your post-launch customer engagement strategy.

Owned Media

Of the three media types, owned media is the most important because you have the most control over it. It's also the place where you should be driving customers and prospects with your paid and earned media efforts. Owned media are the channels that you control: your website, mobile sites, blogs, Twitter, Facebook, LinkedIn, YouTube, and LBS pages.

The goal of your owned media should be to build longer-term relationships with your customers. Your owned media is also a home base for all of your efforts, so as social tools change and evolve, your customers know where to find your best content, tools, products, contact info, and general information about your business.

Owned media must engage your customers just as much as social media. Include information about your company's products and services so potential customers can get a feel for what your company does. You're competing with other conversations and content from people (friends, family, coworkers) who are likely much more interesting to your customers. Your content should be educational and sometimes conversational and even humorous.

Keep an eye on what customers are saying when they check into your venue: the tips they leave, any pictures they post, and the societies, trips, and adventures they create. These updates are a cross between owned and earned media because the comments and content are activity on your turf, and that's a good thing (assuming it's mostly positive). Incorporate any of these into your owned media.

Thread your LBS activity into your website. Many LBS providers give you relatively straightforward application programming interfaces (APIs): Advanced data feeds allow you to thread recent tips, comments, pictures, and other activity into your web page, Twitter stream, or Facebook Page. We also talk more about integrating LBS events into your website in the upcoming section, "Integrating Your Website and Blog." If you don't have the ability to do this in-house, most good web developers know how to work with APIs.

Integrating Facebook and Twitter

It's always a good thing to encourage your customers to cross-post their check-ins from an LBS, such as foursquare, to Facebook and Twitter. The more people who read about your business and location-based campaigns, the better. In some ways, Twitter is a better place to cross-post LBS check-ins than Facebook. Twitter is more searchable than Facebook and is less personal. If you want to reply to a customer, you don't need to be following that customer first whereas on Facebook, you need to be "friends" with someone before you can post on their wall or in some cases, to see their updates.

✔ **Simply ask your customers to cross-post their check-ins.**

With services like Gowalla, you can write a greeting in advance that pops up when a customer checks in. Offer an incentive to cross-post — for example, 10 percent off any merchandise in your store for cross-posting a check-in.

Consider a tiered offer that gives your customers something for checking in, something extra for checking in and cross-posting to Facebook, and something extra special for cross-posting to Facebook and Twitter.

✔ **Advertise in other venues besides social media destinations.**

Add a sign in your store, include details in the message customers hear when you put them on hold, in any of your brochures and printed marketing pieces, or even in your advertising, including your Yellow Pages submission. We talk more about offline advertising in Chapter 16.

✔ **Add a link to your foursquare or Gowalla page on Facebook or Twitter.**

Include links on your bio or background image.

✔ **Code your links into an application programming interface (API).**

You need some technical skills (or resources). APIs are readily available with a little searching. foursquare makes its API available at `https://developer.foursquare.com/`. Figure 8-5 shows an application used for tracking mileage leveraging foursquare's API.

Figure 8-5:
This application uses foursquare's API to track mileage for expense reports.

Facebook includes iFrames, which allow you to pull in code from another site. Using iFrames in a feed from your website or directly from your LBS's API can allow for some cool functionality.

Because Twitter has a simpler interface than Facebook, you can't get as fancy with APIs or iFrames. However, you can use the API to syndicate customer tips, photos, and even a change in mayor into your Twitter stream.

✔ **List your LBS efforts on your Facebook Info tab.**

Even if your customers don't know what Gowalla, SCVNGR, or foursquare are, they can easily click to find that information.

Integrating Your Website and Blog

While Facebook and Twitter provide access to hundreds of millions of potential customers, you are limited in what you can do by their user interfaces, functionalities, and, ultimately, terms of service. To that end, it's easier to connect with customers on your website or blog. After all, you own your website and blog and control all the content.

The advantage of incorporating your LBS campaign into your website provides a few benefits to your company, including these:

✔ **Increased website traffic:** It can allow customers to check in right from your website, which is a great boon if you're running a business that doesn't have a brick-and-mortar location.

✔ **Reviews and other helpful information:** Customers can see tips and comments from other customers. These can serve as the mini-equivalent of Yelp reviews or more formal social commerce functionality that you get from ratings and reviews.

✔ **Hot tips and deals:** You can alert your customers to specials that you want them to have access to before the general public gets that information. This could involve a multiple-step customer activity such as finding a code on your website or blog and entering it after customers check in.

✔ **Custom badges:** Incorporate custom badges that let customers know that you are on a particular LBS (or several).

Include your own videos instructional videos on topics like "what is foursquare?" or "why did we decide to go with the service that we chose?" — or even "we're looking for your feedback on our offers; how are we doing?"

If you produce shows, write books, or create any other kind of nonvenue-based content, consider including your products on http://getglue.com. This service allows people to check into shows, books, magazines, and other nonlocation-based items. Even better, they can comment as they check in and then cross-post that check-in to Twitter or Facebook.

Chapter 9

Using Location in Marketing Beyond the Check-in

In This Chapter

▶ Staking claim to your places on the web

▶ Using location on the web

▶ Advertising on the mobile web

*W*hen people think of location-based services, they often associate it with the check-in, primarily because it is the hot new idea that is capturing the imagination of smart businesses, brands, and marketers. We've talked throughout this book about how location-based services like Gowalla, SCVNGR, Yelp, and others allow someone to express "I am here" with a check-in. We talk a great deal about mobile applications that run on smartphones because these represent a big opportunity to get to know your audience. But there are other platforms that also use location.

People are searching for and planning vacations using Google. They're looking for directions at home, at work, and on vacation on Bing. They're choosing specific experiences based on their location. And there are ways to make it so your business stands out during the process. In this chapter, we take a look at some ways to make your place stand out online.

Using Place to Your Advantage

You can claim your place on many services — even non-LBS ones — and leverage it to enhance the experience of a potential customer searching for your business. People search for places not only on mobile phones, but also through search engines and map applications. You can control the information that they receive in the search results.

Think about how often you use Google Maps and Bing Maps to search for businesses. When a person finds your business on one of these services, the first thing they see is the location pinpointed on the map, with links to additional information on the left side of the page and a box when they hover over the pinpoint. Clicking More Info in Google Maps or clicking the listing in Bing Maps takes them to the business's directory page.

Make an investment in creating and keeping these pages relatively current. Check in on them periodically to make sure that you aren't having problems with customers or prospects. Use any problems as an opportunity to show the public how you respond to issues. Often, you can turn loud adversaries into advocates.

Using Google

Google is the most-often-used search engine, so it's important that your business listing is easily searchable. In fact, one in five searches on Google includes a location aspect — for example, *Indian restaurant Boston.*

In the following sections, we talk about some of the various location-based services Google offers.

Google Places

Enter Google Places: a directory listing of your business that displays photos, reviews, and essential facts about your business (such as address, phone number, and hours), as well as real-time updates and any offers that a customer can take advantage of.

A Google Places page connects several Google experiences to your business, two of them being Google and Google Maps. If you want to capture the on-the-go customer who's searching with a smartphone, Google Places is a service you need to keep up to date. Go to `www.google.com/places` to claim your Google Places listing.

You have some level of control over the content of these elements:

✔ **Organic searches:** You can influence what people searching for your business find in the search results, including your business name, contact information hours, payment types, and the categories associated with your business.

✔ **Map searches:** You can influence what information people get when searching Google Maps, including your phone number, hours of operation, and website address. Figure 9-1 shows a business listing for a Google Maps search. To get more information about a particular business, you click the link in the business. That business's Google Place page appears, as shown in Figure 9-2.

✔ **Google Places ratings:** Customers can leave reviews and ratings. Users can get recommendations and rate restaurants based on their preferences. Be sure to check what people are saying about your business. Spend time responding to reviews. Thank people for praise and make an effort to understand why people are having problems. Actions like this generate goodwill, build advocacy, and encourage people who are already vocal to be more vocal about your business.

Here are the location-based features to look into on Google Places:

✔ **Show which geographic area you do business in.**

If you're a service-oriented business — say, a plumber — where you travel to serve customers, you can show which areas you serve. And if you run a business without a storefront or office location, you can make your address private.

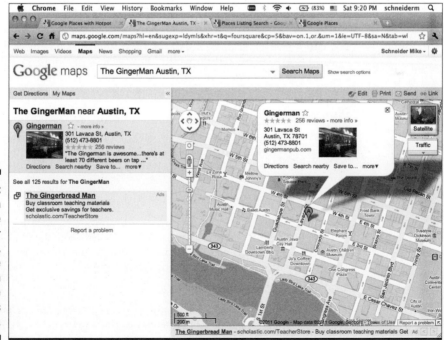

Figure 9-1: When people search for a location, one possible destination is the Google Places page.

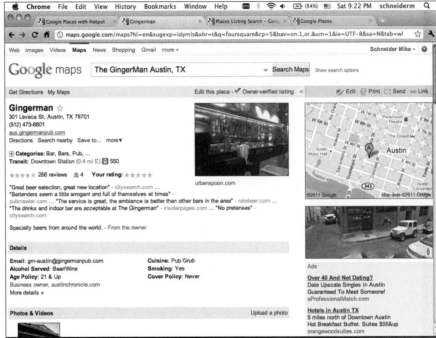

Figure 9-2:
The Austin
Ginger
Man's
Google
Places
Page.

✔ **Incorporate additional advertising.**

You can make your listing stand out on Google and Google Maps with tags. *Tags* are yellow markers that allow you to promote an important part of your business. Unlike the rest of the Google Places features, this one isn't free. We talk more about Tags in the next section.

✔ **Show photos.**

You can upload your own photos, and also request a free photo shoot of the interior of your business to supplement your existing photos. Go to `http://maps.google.com/help/maps/businessphotos` for more info.

✔ **Offer customized QR codes to your customers.**

You can download a *QR code* (a bar code) unique to your business. You can place your QR codes on your business cards or other marketing materials, and customers can scan them with smartphones that take them to the mobile version of your Place Page.

✔ **Advertise via favorite places.**

If your business gains enough popularity on Google Places (determined by Google via how many hits your Places Page gets) Google will send you a window decal to place in the window of your store. Your decal includes a QR code that a customer can scan with a smartphone to view your mobile Place Page and find out more about your offerings.

✔ **Post real-time updates.**

If you're promoting a sale, a special event, or anything else that you want customers to know right now, you can communicate that directly to your customers. You can also provide extra incentive by adding coupons (maybe your current LBS offer), including ones specially formatted for mobile phones.

With Google Places, you get a Google Analytics–style dashboard that shows how much activity you're getting on your page. Here's a list of the helpful metrics that you can get:

✔ **Impressions:** This is how many times someone saw your page. Impressions are indicative of how often people search for your business.

✔ **Actions:** How many times a user showed some kind of interest in your page. This can be further broken down into:

- *Clicks for more information on the map:* The searcher found your Google Places pages and clicked on Google information. In other words, they didn't click through to your site.

- *Clicks for driving directions:* A good measure of a person's intent.

- *Clicks to your website:* The searcher likes you enough to get more information.

✔ **Top search queries:** The Google Places dashboard page also shows you the top search queries that led people to your Places page.

✔ **Driving directions:** Shows you what zip codes the people who are requesting directions to your place are coming from, based on the Get Directions From field.

Note that Google Places doesn't give you personally identifying information about the people who come to your page.

Google Boost

Google Boost allows you to extend the capabilities of your Google Places account; you can buy keywords that will drive a user to your Google Places page. The search results appear on the map with a blue icon, as shown in Figure 9-3. (If this book were printed in color, you'd see that the A pinpoint displays in blue while all other pinpoints are red. Also notice that the business listing for blue pinpoint A, The Auto Repair Experts, appears near the top of the page in the area designated for paid advertising.) You can display your address, phone number, and a one-line ad. The blue pin stands out in a sea of red ones. Google Boost ads appear on both web and mobile searches.

A paid ad using Google Boost

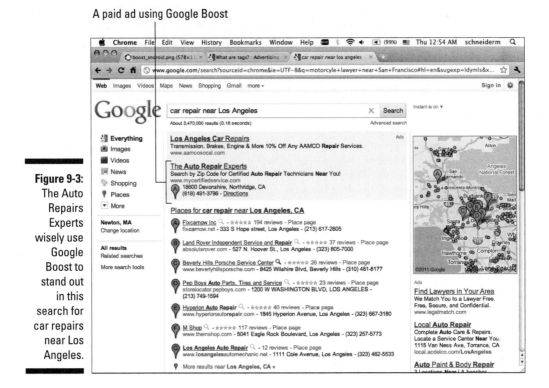

Figure 9-3:
The Auto
Repairs
Experts
wisely use
Google
Boost to
stand out
in this
search for
car repairs
near Los
Angeles.

Google Boost will cost you some money. Go to www.google.com/boost for more information, including pricing.

Targeting with Twitter Places

Twitter has a feature called Places that allows you to geotag a tweet with your current location. Twitter grabs your location and appends it to your tweets.

You can then analyze tweets by geography. This is particularly useful if you are a "regional" brand looking to engage with customers in a particular area. Twitter also uses geodata to decide who it sends a promoted tweet or promoted user. *Promoted tweets* are tweets that have been paid for, and you find them on your Twitter stream regardless of whether you're following the brand. *Promoted users* are suggested in the People You Should Follow section.

If you pay for Twitter ads (promoted tweets or promoted user accounts), you gain access to the Twitter Follower Dashboard. The dashboard gives you a look at the following:

- ✔ **Engagement:** The percentage of people who have seen your tweet and the number of people who have retweeted, replied, or favorited your tweets.

- ✔ **Location:** This treemap shows a breakdown of people who tweet with you by location. The chart starts at the country level and breaks it down in one chart.

- ✔ **Your Followers Also Follow:** A list of who your followers also follow.

- ✔ **Gender:** A pie chart that shows the breakdown of Twitter users that follow you by male, female and unknown.

- ✔ **Interests:** Gives you the percentage of followers interested in various topics like news, tech, social media, burritos, and so on.

- ✔ **Follower Graph:** A graph that shows the growth of your Twitter account followers.

These give you a chance to target messages to geographies, genders, and even interests. Costs for promoted tweets range between ten and fifty cents cost-per-engagement at time of print. There is also a cost-per-follower charge that starts at .50 and tops out at $2.00 per follower attached to a promoted user account.

Use the geotagging options to find people close by that you can develop relationships with through conversations. Buying followers gives you more followers, but it does not necessarily give you the right followers. You want to find people who share your brand's interests and who you can eventually do business with.

Yelp

Yelp is an enormous social network dedicated to helping people find businesses that they will like. Yelp's secret is its user-generated content. Users can log in to Yelp; find your business by location, category, or name of the business, and write a review. It's free to claim your business at biz.yelp.com. If you need to do so, turn to Chapter 4.

Yelp is powerful, but it's not perfect. If your business is complex, reviews can be confusing. Green Tea, shown in Figure 9-4, has two kinds of cuisine, but only one rating.

Figure 9-4:
It's hard
to judge
reviews by
the aggre-
gate rating.

Ratings in Yelp are very important because search results are typically arranged first by cuisine type, then geography, followed by rating from best to worst. Other attributes include the phone number, information on reservations, online reservations using OpenTable, parking, attire, price ranger, good for kids.

Most people aren't taking the subtleties and complexities of restaurants into consideration when they are making their decisions. Some people just look at the overall score. Others read the top review. Very few people actually dig deep into the reviews and read them all. This is one of the disadvantages of crowd sourced content.

As a marketer, you can't ignore Yelp. 38 million users are reviewing your business whether or not they are qualified to, and people are using this information to make decisions. The web site gets about 14 million unique visitors a month and that does not include mobile. Only Yelp and the users have the ability to make a change to a negative review, so if you see one, you should do what you can to resolve the issue with the customer who had a problem. Figure 9-5 shows a Yelp review with a link to send a message to the reviewer.

Figure 9-5: Clicking a user's profile will allow you to send them a message.

Click this link to send a message.

Yelp also has an advertising model that allows you to put pictures on your page and highlight reviews that you like. You can also activate Open Table so that people can make online reservations (if you are a restaurant). The advertising premise is similar to search engine advertising where you can bid to get your business featured in search results. In other words, it will take precedence over anything that would have organically been seen as more relevant by the search engine.

Organic search results are those that would be returned by a search algorithm (program) without any outside influence. Paid results are bought by purchasing keywords from the search engine.

Bing Local

www.bing.com/businessportal

Bing is Microsoft's search engine, a competitor of Google. Compete.com, a tool that tracks the amount of traffic to websites, reported in January 2011 that Bing had 29 percent of searches.

Bing has its own version of Google Places called Bing Local (sign up for a Live Windows ID to get access). Bing Business Portal allows you to do things like tailor or correct the information about your business, submit your website's site map so that Bing has a better idea of how to crawl your site and it also allows you access to search engine marketing. The results appear in Bing and Bing Local. Customers can also make a reservation using OpenTable through Bing Local (see Figure 9-6).

You actually have a great deal of control over your listing, through the dashboard (see Figure 9-7).

- ✔ **Details:** Specify your address and phone number, web addresses, your Facebook account, Twitter account, your logo, and other special purpose phone numbers, websites, and e-mails.

- ✔ **Profile:** Specify the type of business you are from multiple categories. There is a cool variable bar chart that you can use to specify how dedicated your organization is to a particular category as well.

- ✔ **Mobile:** Create a free mobile website. It's a pretty rudimentary way to put your products and specials (also defined in that tab) online.

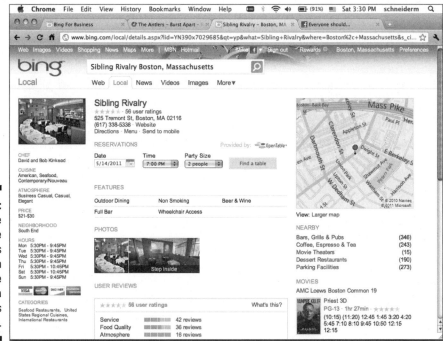

Figure 9-6:
People make reservations through OpenTable through a Bing Places page.

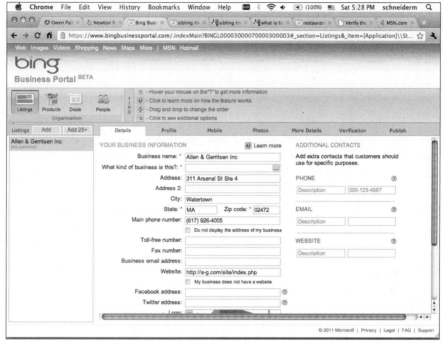

Figure 9-7:
The Bing
Business
Portal
dashboard
gives you a
great deal of
control over
your mes-
sage in Bing
Local.

 ✔ **Photos:** Add up to 9 photos that you want people to see on your company page.

Photos give potential customers a sense of what your business is like, so
make sure that the photos are bright, clean, and demonstrate a positive
experience.

 ✔ **More Details:** Give an even deeper dive into your organization from the
year established and company tagline, to a description of your business,
languages spoken, brands carried, professional affiliations, and a chance
to tweak your placement on the map.

GPS-Driven Advertising

Some mobile advertising networks are digital advertising platforms for
mobile. They allow you to buy placements on mobile websites. When you
buy placements, you get to put your ad in that spot for a given period of time.

Some technologies allow you to buy location-specific advertisements.
Networks like Navteq Locationpoint and WHERE (formerly uLocate) allow
you to target people in places where they are using GPS technology across
GPS navigation devices like Garmin and TomTom, smartphones, and tablets.

Ad networks collect advertisements from advertisers and match them to a series of requirements on publisher's sites. This is largely standardized on the (non-mobile) web because the delivery methods are standard: HTML, HTML5, or Flash. The mobile web uses a totally different paradigm with both mobile web technologies (WAP, HTML, and HTML5) and app-based computing over multiple operating systems on Apple, Microsoft, Android, and other smartphones.

So you can imagine that these networks need to deliver ads via not only the web but specific applications. This makes buying mobile ads a lot more fragmented than buying ads for the (non-mobile) web. Therefore you need to find ways to buy ads for navigation devices separate from mobiles devices and often for specific applications.

For example, in the case of Navteq, you advertise on GPS devices because Navteq has built an ad network into the operating system. When it comes to phones, Navteq built an application called Poynt, a local search engine similar to Yelp.

Mobile advertising requires more time and planning than advertising on the web.

Part IV
Measuring Your Return on Investment

The 5th Wave   By Rich Tennant

"I hope you're doing something online. A group like yours shouldn't just be playing street corners."

In this part . . .

For all you measurement and analytics types, Part IV is a must-read. In this part, we help you set key performance indicators and use dashboards and measurement techniques for location-based marketing campaigns.

In this part, you find out about

- ✔ Connecting the dots between location-based activity and return on investment (ROI)
- ✔ Unlocking the power of your advocates and most loyal fans
- ✔ Learning about monitoring the social web

Chapter 10

Setting Up a Monitoring Strategy

There are glorious opportunities available today to learn about what your audience is saying about you. Your audience is anyone who is — or you want to be — listening to you. In other words, as a business, your audience includes your customers and prospects.

Big data and social media are the keys to gaining insights that you can then use to capture more customers. People are sharing more data than they ever have, and it's not just "I am here." Your audience will tell you about their ideas, their work, their passions. They can interact with you. They're questioning, exploring, advocating, and complaining.

The first step to measurement is *monitoring:* gathering, surfing, and getting to know your data. *Measurement* is a rigorous application of metrics, formulas, and algorithms to scientifically make a determination. We talk about monitoring in this chapter; we go into detail about measuring in Chapter 11.

To find out more about monitoring via the social web, pick up a copy of *Social Media Marketing For Dummies,* by Shiv Singh.

Defining Your Monitoring Strategy

Monitoring is the act of setting up a series of actions that allows you to search the web for pieces of data that help tell a meaningful story for your business. Owned and earned media like blogs, websites, Facebook (sometimes), Twitter, and even some location-based services can be monitored by tools that comb the web for insights that are specific to your business.

Your job as a marketer is to build a strategy to decipher or measure the messages that you find and turn them into information that can build relationships with prospects and customers and ultimately give you an advantage over your competition.

Deciding what to monitor

When setting up your strategy, consider monitoring the following categories:

- ✔ **Brand name:** The most important thing to watch for is your brand name. Your brand mentions are signals that someone cares enough to mention something about your business.

- ✔ **Your competitors' brand names:** One of the great things that social monitoring can do for you is give you competitive intelligence. You get to see not only who is talking about your brand, but you see what people are saying about your competitors' brands. If people are complaining about them, you can offer solutions with your brand. If people are praising the other brands, you can see if your brand can fulfill the same promises.

- ✔ **Complementary businesses:** Watch for opportunities to do more business. For example, airports, coffee shops, restaurants and bars can all have customers that can become your customers. Tourists are looking for things to do, and visiting your business could be one of those things.

- ✔ **Partners' brand names:** It's also helpful to monitor the brand names of any potential partners so that you can get a sense of their reputations before you work with them. Because people often talk about customer service issues, this will give you some insight into your partner's strengths and weaknesses. You might even be so bold as to converse with people who are having issues to get to the root of the problems.

- ✔ **Admired brands:** Whether in your industry or not, there are probably brands that you would like to model your brand after. Watching these brands will show you how they conduct themselves and inspire your content strategy.

- ✔ **Products:** Sometimes people don't mention your brand name when they talk about your products, but you want to hear what they're saying. People talk about innovative uses for your products, they praise them, they tell you what's wrong, and sometimes they compare them directly to your competition, so it's wise to follow the discussion of your products in social media.

- ✔ **Offers:** If you want to know if your competition is using social media for offers, you can find them by listening for them. Some brands use social media for nothing but offers.

Social media isn't just another broadcast channel; it's an opportunity to get to know your audience and provide value to them beyond what they get from your products and services.

✔ **Brand pillar–related conversations:** Your brand stands for something—pillars. Example pillars are health, adventure, sustainability, and quality. People tend to act like brands, and brands act like people. For this to happen, you need to extract the *passion points* (for example: Hannaford Supermarket's are "easy, healthy, and affordable") from your brand. You usually derive these from your brand pillars. They invite you into conversations that expand your ability to communicate with your audience. For instance, if you're running a marketing campaign for a skateboard company, constantly talking about your *deck* (boards) and apparel will get stale pretty fast. If you take a step back and provide quality content for people based on the ideals of your brand, you'll find more opportunities for interaction.

✔ **Campaigns:** Use social media monitoring to gain intelligence that will give you campaign-generating ideas. Say you operate a craft brewery, and you're interested in launching a new amber ale. Social monitoring allows you to comb the web for the conversations about amber ales, which gives you ideas on how to model your campaign. You'll find breweries, experts, enthusiasts, beer geeks, newbies, and nonbelievers having conversations about beers like Anderson Valley's Boont Amber Ale, Ballast Point's Calico Amber, Tröegs's HopBack Amber Ale, and more in owned and earned media.

Setting your frequency

The more you pay attention to your activity streams the better. Monitoring gives back when you put in time and effort. While most people say that you should listen, measure, and engage, a lot of brands don't realize that the more you engage, the more you have to listen and measure. Dedicate full-time resources to community management — if you can — both on your site and in earned media spaces.

Work your location-based marketing into your workflow. Treat it as you do checking e-mail, taking phone calls, or talking to customers in your store. Ultimately you need to decide how much time you dedicate to monitoring. If you're a smaller business, make it the job of everyone and be sure to make it a part of your daily internal dialogue.

Finding insight in your searches

You will find tweets, blog posts, Facebook statuses and conversations, check-ins, articles, pictures, and news from a myriad of sites. Some search engines are even aggregating public check-ins from Gowalla and question data from Quora. This means that social data is gaining even more importance and prominence with Google.

Here are some examples of insights that brands have received from social media monitoring. We also note the platform (paid tool) that the brand used to get the information.

The American Red Cross

Platform: Radian6

Social media listening is viable as an early warning system in a crisis. The resulting information may inspire people to act quickly. Social media can be used to collect donations, triage situations, reach officials and eyewitnesses, or simply tell the story from ground zero.

In January 2010, a devastating earthquake hit Haiti. The American Red Cross was one of the first to respond and disseminate information. They had to know right away what information to share and where to share it.

Because the American Red Cross was monitoring its social media pages before this happened, they understood beforehand that various social networks have various needs. They realized that their Facebook page was a discussion platform and their Twitter account was meant for sending out news, updates, and donation information. They also monitored during the crisis, trying to figure out what the main sentiment of the general public was. They found that most people were asking, "How can I help?" — so they shared information accordingly. During the time of disaster, the Red Cross found that social media was extremely crucial in sharing information.

Dell

Platform: Radian6

You can use social media to turn a negative situation into a positive. In this situation, Dell was burned by social media, but the company managed to turn the situation around.

Brian Lam, a blogger from Gizmodo, ran across Michael Dell carrying a new laptop he had never seen before. It turned out to be the Inspiron 910, the Mini 9, which was scheduled for release in four months. Lam wrote a blog post highlighting the expected product specifications.

Dell monitored what people were saying and gained insight on what customers were most excited about seeing in the new product. Dell was careful to let the conversation happen as organically as possible; however, they ever so often added tidbits of information and corrections to misinformation.

Dell was able to comprehend what customers were expecting as far as features and prices for the new computer and subsequently launched messaging around what they learned. When it came to the actual launch, Dell felt informed and prepared for the launch, and they were excited to build upon the buzz that social media had already generated. During this four-month period, Dell found that, many times, mentions of other Dell products lead to mentions of the Mini 9 as well. They were able to effectively monitor and market the product based on customer wants and expectations.

Mint Social

Platform: Social Mention

You can watch how far a message spreads and whether it travels across social channels. Mint Social did a press release on being named one of the Top 10 social media optimization companies in the U.S. by topseos.com. The press release was picked up on social media, SEO PR channels, and local media channels. Mint Social tracked over 95 online mentions in the first week. They thought this was a good result but that they could also do better. Mint Social tweaked their press release and redistributed it to different channels. They found through social media monitoring that it had 257 additional mentions.

Jason Peck and Major League Baseball

Platform: Valuevine

Jason Peck, author of the blog Take a Peck, wanted to understand how Valuevine could be used to track consumer activity at sporting venues.

To coincide with opening day 2011, Valuevine teamed up with Jason Peck to monitor, measure, and provide analytics and trends for each of the 30 Major League Baseball stadiums for the duration of the 2011 season. They first found all historical data for all the MLB stadiums combined to get a baseline for activity and sentiment. They're also measuring community size, positive sentiment, stadium check-ins, and a comparison of the National League and American League from a consumer activity perspective.

Best Buy

Platform: Scout Labs by Lithium

Social monitoring is a good way to find people who need help. If you build a community for customer service, you might even find that customers like to solve problems for one another.

Best Buy wanted to find a way to engage its audience, provide support, build advocacy, and provide recommendations across multiple channels in a manageable way.

Best Buy began to monitor the blogosphere for customers who needed customer service or technical support and helped resolve their questions or guided them to an answer. In 2008, it launched the Best Buy Community, which allows customers to talk to Best Buy advocates as well as other customers. To make sure customers in all channels were engaged, the team used Twitter in English, Spanish, and French, and created biweekly videos. After this got too difficult to manage, Best Buy partnered with Scout Labs to start the Twelpforce initiative, which allows any authorized team member to respond to questions directly from Twitter. Best Buy sees about 600,000 customers visiting the community and posting 20,000 messages per quarter.

Choosing Monitoring Tools

We can't possibly mention every tool that helps you with monitoring. That topic would easily fill a book of its own. But in the following sections, we discuss a few of the more popular tools.

Google Alerts and Google Trends

Google Alerts (www.google.com/alerts) searches the web for anything you want (in this case, you or your brand) and gives you a list of mentions on the Internet via e-mail. Google Trends (www.google.com/trends) tells you about the macro-level Internet activity for a keyword (as demonstrated in Figure 10-1). You can even compare keywords, and it shows you a trend line over time with milestone articles.

Figure 10-1 shows the Internet mentions of Coke and Pepsi over time.

Remember the following about Internet searches:

- ✔ **The information is not always precise.**

  Coke got a significant bump in May 2010 when a drug lord named Coke escaped from Jamaican forces.

- ✔ **Mentions are by location at the bottom of the page.**

  For instance, the instances of Pepsi in Denver are about 3 to 1 over Coke. Also note the irony of Coke being blue and Pepsi being red in the chart. We didn't get to pick the colors.

Social Mention

Social Mention (http://socialmention.com) is a search engine that crawls more than one hundred social media websites and services, including Twitter, Facebook, FriendFeed, YouTube, Digg, and Google. It allows you to do some segmentation on blogs, microblogs (Twitter, FriendFeed, and so on), book-marking sites (Digg, StumbleUpon, and reddit), comments, events, images, news, video, audio, Q&A, and social networks. It even attempts to tell you how strong the conversation is, the positive-to-negative sentiment ratio, how passionate the audience is, and how far reaching. You can get these results sent to you via e-mail or you can have them piped into your blog via a widget.

Figure 10-2 shows the features of Social Mention in action:

- The 1 percent strength is an indicator that this conversation isn't very vibrant.

- The 3:1 sentiment means that the sentiment in the conversation is 3 times more positive than negative when the sentiment is identifiable.

Sentiment analysis is pretty primitive so take it with a grain of salt. It's pretty tough to know when sentiment is true especially when sarcasm is prevalent on the Internet.

✓ People mention this brand multiple times 24 percent of the time.

Passion attempts to measure how often a person who talks about you repeats it. It doesn't necessarily mean they are positive, but they are doing it.

Reach tells you how many people are involved in the conversation. It's a gauge of how many unique authors are in the conversation. In other words, you would like to get as close to 100% reach and passion as possible with an overwhelming positive sentiment.

Note also that these results can be captured via an RSS feed, which means you can use the results in other applications and that you can also download them to an Excel file for analysis.

Figure 10-2:
A search for skateboard company Loaded's popular longboard the Dervish on Social Mention.

Twitter clients

Twitter clients like HootSuite, TweetDeck, Seesmic, and CoTweet can help you create and build Twitter streams that give you the information that you care about watching. They allow you to build columns that suit specific monitoring needs. You can follow Twitter accounts and create persistent searches (see the upcoming section, "Monitoring Check-ins with Twitter", for more information on how to create a search using Twitter) that pull extremely specific information like your competitors' product information or people checking in to their places. Tweetdeck and Hootsuite also have device clients for the Apple iOS and Google Android.

For example, if you're marketing for an Austin, Texas–area restaurant, you can set up your search criteria on TweetDeck in the following ways (see Figure 10-3):

- **First column:** Displays a list of people checking into the Austin airport. You can then send an offer to these people.
- **Second column:** Monitors your restaurant's check-ins and mentions.
- **Third column:** Tracks a competitor. You can track as many restaurants as you want.

Figure 10-3: Monitoring search columns in TweetDeck.

Choosing a paid tool

Paid tools come in all shapes and sizes. Tools like Radian6 (www.radian6. com), Scout Labs (part of Lithium) (www.lithium.com), BrandsEye (www. brandseye.com), and Visible Technologies (www.visibletechnologies. com) give you a robust set of functions like charts, graphs, word clouds, and so on that you can use to show the impact of social media over time. GeoIQ (www.geoiq.com) is a data visualization tool that allows you to subscribe to social, weather, finance, and government data and juxtapose that with private data like budgets, forecasts, and actuals.

This landscape goes a bit beyond the scope of this book, but these tools are extremely powerful and offer you very extensive data. Paid tools often give you access to far more data than free tools. When choosing them, try to get a sense for how much of a particular platform you're interested in that they can expose. Some of them, for example, can give you only a 30-day window of Twitter data.

Monitoring Check-ins with Twitter

The beauty of social spaces is that people are willing to share things like where they are and what they're eating and drinking. Even better is that they're willing to share it in public. You can monitor your business and brand's activity in many ways on location-based social networks. When someone checks in to your business, most location-based services allow him to push the check-in to Twitter and Facebook.

When people push check-ins to Twitter, those check-ins are pushed using a certain convention. In other words, a place looks the same each time it is pushed to Twitter. This allows you to find check-ins for your business using Twitter's search tool.

Using the Twitter search page is the lowest level of monitoring. It's a good place to test a result, but not the best place to continuously monitor your traffic. For that, you should use a monitoring tool like TweetDeck or HootSuite.

The first thing to do is find the people who are checking in to your place. Follow these steps:

1. **Go to http://search.twitter.com.**

   The Twitter Search page opens, as shown in Figure 10-4.

2. **Enter your search criteria in the See What's Happening box.**

Figure 10-4:
Searching
Twitter.

3. **(Optional) Click the Advanced Search button to perform a more in-depth search.**

    We talk about how to use operators to come up with a very detailed query in the next section.

4. **Click Search.**

    The results are limited to a short window of time, so you should repeat these steps over the course of your monitoring strategy.

To capture any data that you want to keep from a search requires you to create a database to capture the tweets. If this is too advanced for you, you can hire a company that does custom application and database development. Agencies will also often help you build custom solutions.

Creating structured queries

Each query allows you to use a bunch of cool operators. We keep things simple here, but you can create some pretty fancy queries once you understand how to use operators. Here are the tips for creating useful queries in the Twitter search engine:

✔ **All-or-nothing** Type your search criteria into the search box and click Search returns results that contain all the words you type. This example

```
Dervish longboard
```

returns results that have both the words "dervish" and "longboard" and not necessarily in order or together. Figure 10-5 shows these results.

✔ **Precise phrase** Wrap a phrase in quotes to find that exact phrase returned in search results. For example

```
"independent trucks"
```

returns anything that includes those two words together.

However,

```
independent trucks
```

returns all results that have "independent" and "trucks" appearing some-where, not necessarily together. Figure 10-6 shows the different results you get.

✔ **OR** The OR operator returns one phrase *or* another; it's a way to combine search terms. Say you're a skateboard manufacturer and you want to look at a bunch of competitive brands. Use the OR operator in this way:

```
Loaded OR Rayne OR "Sector 9" OR "Santa Cruz" OR Honey
        OR Palisades
```

Figure 10-5: Searching for Dervish longboard ensures both words are in the results.

Figure 10-6:
Columns two and three have subtle differences in search construction that yield different results.

You get results that have "Loaded," "Rayne," "Sector 9," and "Santa Cruz" appearing somewhere. You could find an article that mentions "Loaded" but not any of the other terms and vice versa.

✔ - Insert a hyphen (the *not including* operator) in front of a search term to exclude a term from your search results. Use it when you want to narrow a topic and take out things that have no interest to you. For instance, if you want to monitor beer conversations but you're not interested in some specific brands, use the not including operator in this way:

```
__beer -Bud -Budweiser -Coors -Schlitz -Busch
```

All of your results will mention "beer," but you get only results that don't mention "Bud," Budweiser," "Coors," "Schlitz," or "Busch."

✔ # Hashtags are special ways to tag a tweet. They start with a pound (#) sign and relate tweets assuming that people have decided to use the hashtag. For example, if you want to search for tweets about South by Southwest (SXSW), the music, film, and technology conference, use the hashtag operator like this:

```
#SXSW
```

You can also combine terms to get specific content. This example searches for SXSW at the PepsiCo Stage or Pepsi Max lot:

```
#SXSW OR "PepsiCo" OR #pepsicostage OR #pepsimax OR @
     pepsimax
```

✔ **to:, from:, and @** A "to" is the Twitter account that receives a tweet. This usually means that the account is the first thing tweeted. In other words, the @reply (*@account name*) is the first thing in the tweet. A "from" is a tweet from the sender.

This example returns all tweets that Mike Schneider received. His name is listed first in the tweet:

```
to:schneidermike
```

This example returns all tweets that Aaron Strout sent from his account:

```
from:aaronstrout
```

This example finds all tweets that reference Eric Leist's account:

```
@ericleist
```

The three different results are shown in Figure 10-7.

Searching for the account name returns tweets that reference that account name whether the account owner was the person that the tweet was intended for.

Figure 10-7:
Column one
has all
tweets to
@Schneider-
Mike.
Column
two is only
tweets sent
by @Aaron-
Strout.
Column three
is tweets
referencing
@EricLeist.

✔ **near: and within:** Many tweets are *geotagged,* meaning that a location has been appended to a tweet. These locations are usually not specific places unless the tweet text is an LBS check-in. They are tagged with a city and state or region and country.

The following returns all geotagged tweets within 15 miles of New York City:

```
near:NYC within:15mi
```

Note that you aren't required to use `within:` in combination with `near:`. You can use `near:` alone.

✔ **since: and until:** When you're searching for tweets, you may want to search for them within a certain time frame. (Just note that tweets don't last forever, so you may not find tweets from, say, April 12, 2006.)

In this case, `since:` is a beginning date, and `until:` is an end date. Dates need to be formed in a *yyyy-mm-dd* format where *y* = year, *m* = month, and *d* = day.

This gives you all tweets starting on January 1, 2010.

```
From:2010-01-01
```

Search for everything prior to September 21, 2011

```
Until:2011-09-21
```

✔ **Sentiment** The official documents of Twitter Search say that you can use emoticons like :) and :(to determine positive and negative attitudes in a tweet respectively. What actually happens is that the search engine pulls out tweets tagged with those emoticons. That's a good start but it's not perfect. Sentiment (positive and negative) analysis is hard to get right. Things like sarcasm get in the way of perfection.

Here is an example. You can find positive tweets about Gowalla by using this search construction:

```
Gowalla :)
```

Sentiment (positive vs. negative feeling) is really hard to gauge in a tweet because of things like sarcasm, so use these at your own peril.

✔ **filter:links** This allows you to find results with (or without) links.

For example, conversations about Brooklyn indie rock band Neon Indian that include links can tell you what services people are using to listen to Neon Indian and also what songs they like. Use these search terms and operators:

```
"Neon Indian" filter:links
```

If you want to see the result without links, simply add not including (-) operator as follows:

```
"Neon Indian" -filter:links
```

Finding check-in data

People always have the option to cross-post check-ins from location-based services to twitter. Because Twitter is a public space, you can see what people post. This gives you the opportunity to monitor who is checking in at your place as well as competitors and neighbors. To do that, you need to know a little about how the data is structured so that when you search, you get the results you want.

To find check-ins to your business, you have to do a little research on your venue in foursquare, Gowalla, Yelp, and SCVNGR (for example) to see how it is named. Your business also might not be listed the same way on each platform. Figure 10-8 shows how one restaurant is listed several different ways on Gowalla. This is because for most of these platforms, the places are generated by users. Users do not really care about data standards, so you often see a variation — 99 represented as 99, Ninety Nine, Ninety-Nine, or perhaps even Nine Nine.

Every service has a database of places, called the *places database*. The places database lists each variation of your business name; you need to search for each variation to extract all the data pertaining to your business. Gowalla and foursquare have their own databases. SCVNGR uses Google Places.

Doing this search is most critical when your business has an informal name or includes numbers.

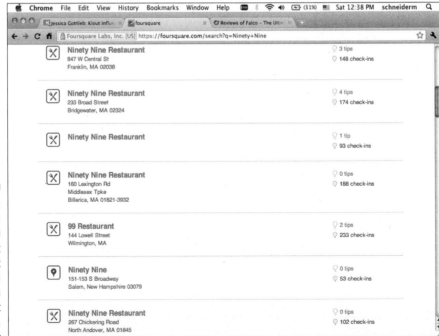

Figure 10-8:
A search for the 99 Restaurant reveals that some venue names aren't standard.

When you know how your business is listed, you can then start to build a search query on Twitter. But you need one more piece of information. Each location-based service gives each of your names listed in its places database a specific URL, which is then used when someone pushes a check-in to other services (such as Facebook and Twitter). To find that check-in on Twitter, you need to know that URL.

> ✔ Gowalla uses *gowal.la*.
>
> ✔ foursquare uses *4sq.com*.
>
> ✔ SCVNGR *scvn.gr*.

Now you can build a query using the OR operator that gets all of your check-ins from Twitter.

```
Uncle Billy's gowal.la OR 4sq.com OR svn.gr
```

Figure 10-9 shows the check-ins for Uncle Billy's BBQ in Austin, TX as a result of this query. Notice a mix of both foursquare and Gowalla check-ins. There aren't any SCVNGR check-ins displaying, but if anyone checks in on SCVNGR, it will show in the results.

You can type this into Twitter Search to get a one time results set or you can create a column in Twitter, TweetDeck, HootSuite, or Seesmic to continuously monitor the results. These searches are portable across multiple clients. They all use the same search syntax.

Type your business name exactly as it is saved in the application's places database. Search queries are exact. If your place name isn't the same across the various LBS databases, edit it so your name is uniform across all the services. You'll save yourself from complicated queries. Turn to Chapter 5 to find out how to edit your information.

If you have multiple venues and want to monitor them individually, or you want to monitor specific competitor places, you need to build your search with the exact name of the place you want to track. For instance, Zoka Coffee is in Seattle and nearby cities. Suppose you want to monitor check-ins to the Kirkland location only. A quick search on Twitter for Zoka Coffee shows several ways to searching for it, but that the one in Kirkland looks like this:

```
Zoka Coffee (129 Central Way, Kirkland)
```

So if you want to isolate your search for foursquare check-ins to Zoka Coffee in Kirkland, WA use:

```
Zoka Coffee (129 Central Way, Kirkland) 4sq.com
```

Figure 10-10 shows the results for this query.

Figure 10-9:
A search for check-ins for Uncle Billy's Brew & Que in Austin, TX.

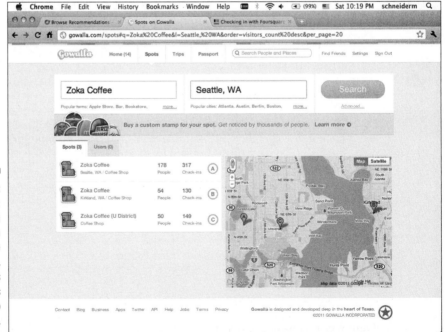

Figure 10-10:
Zoka Coffee in Washington has multiple locations, but this search is limited to Kirkland.

You're only getting a sample of people — those who choose to push their check-ins. This isn't an accurate representation of the total number of people checking it. For that, you need to a measurement tool. See Chapter 12.

Watching your competitor's traffic

Tracking competitive check-ins is simple: Simply swap your business name for theirs. Figure 10-11 shows the search results from a query tracking competitors of a barbecue restaurant using TweetDeck.

Figure 10-11: Set up TweetDeck to monitor your competitors.

Understanding When to Respond and How

Influencers are people who check into your places often, tell people in their social networks about your business, and pass on your deals and content. Finding these people is getting easier all the time because people like to use free, open tools (such as Facebook and Twitter) to propagate their check-ins and recommendations.

When you find an influencer, you can leverage that person's *social graph* (network of people that they follow and who follow them) to your advantage. You have many more people to listen to and monitor.

When someone checks in to your business, look at her profile. It's rich in statistics. If you're using Twitter to monitor check-ins, you can click the username to learn more about her. This will take you to her Twitter profile. When looking at Twitter, first look at how many followers she has and how many tweets. You can read her profile and get a sense of what she likes to talk about. Then you can thank her for checking in and start a conversation.

Figure 10-12 shows the Twitter feed for Tara Hunt, known as @missrogue. She has a significant following and tweets fairly often. If she pushes a check-in to her Twitter stream, you can bet a lot of people will see it. If she checks in to your business, you might want to talk to her. Use Twitter to ask her if everything was to her liking. If it wasn't, find out how it could be improved, fix the problem, and invite her back when you've done so. Take every chance to turn a negative into a positive.

Klout (`http://klout.com`) gives you an idea of the kind of tweeter a person is. Klout's segmentation strategy defines tweeters as explorers, specialists, celebrities, taste makers, and more.

Don't put a lot of stock in a Klout score — it's more for entertainment purposes — but the segments can give a reasonable explanation of how a user uses Twitter.

Figure 10-12:
Tara Hunt
has 36,457
followers,
making her
influential.

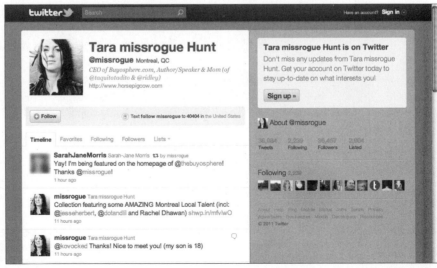

Courtesy of Tara E. Hunt

Here's how a restaurant owner, for example, can use Klout: Imagine you see @jessicagottlieb check in to your business. (She loves dim sum and pho.) Look her up on Klout (as shown in Figure 10-13), and then reach out and ask her what she had to eat. She'll probably answer you, and she'll definitely tell you if it was good enough. Next time she comes in, give her some free nai huang bao to thank her for introducing her friends to you via the check-in that she pushed to her Twitter account.

Responding to customers and prospects is something you have to get used to doing as part of your daily operations. Responding to customers reasonably goes a long way. The easiest way to respond is to look for questions. In location-based marketing, this means looking for people who are asking you for something. You can try giving it to them and see if they come back.

Keep these tips in mind when responding:

 ✔ **Customers expect to be respected.**

   They want to be heard, and they want to be treated like they're valuable. If you give them a chance to talk to you, they'll engage in a dialogue. They will give you ideas about how your business can be more effective, and many of them actually like you enough to do it for free.

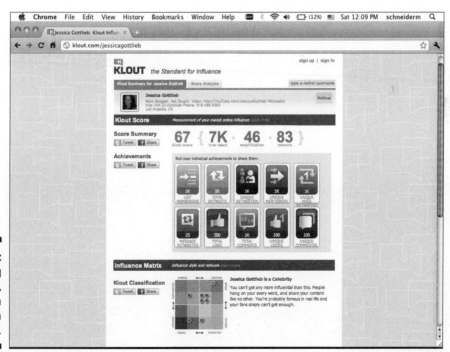

Figure 10-13:
According to Klout, Jessica Gottlieb is a Celebrity.

Courtesy of Jessica Gottlieb

Make a policy to always respect your customers. A little goodwill goes a long way.

✔ **The best time not to respond is when you stop caring.**

✔ **The best channel to use is the one that the customer first contacted you on.**

If that channel lacks an engagement model, default to Twitter or Facebook. Gowalla, foursquare, and SCVNGR all have ways to engage with people who are checked in. Test them out, but note that it's harder to capture and measure conversations on LBS than it is on Twitter and Facebook.

Chapter 11

Setting Your Location-Based Key Performance Indicators

K ey performance indicators (KPI) is just a fancy way of saying "key metrics." You're probably already familiar with some KPIs for your business, such as year-over-year sales growth, net profit, gross sales, customer retention, and employee efficiency. In this chapter, we get specific about KPIs for your location-based marketing.

Determining Your Campaign Key Performance Indicators (KPIs)

Having goals for your campaign is key to achieving measurable success. You can derive your location-based KPIs from your existing business goals.

Here are some things you can measure to incorporate into your campaign's KPIs; track the number of each of the following elements:

- ✔ Daily check-ins
- ✔ New check-ins
- ✔ Employee check-ins
- ✔ Check-ins cross-posted to Twitter
- ✔ Check-ins cross-posted to Facebook
- ✔ Unique check-ins

- Comments and tips
- Photos
- Deals redeemed from specials nearby
- Promoters (people that would recommend your business)
- Detractors (people that would not promote your business)
- Frequency of check-ins

These data points offer a wealth of information. For instance, if click-through rates of specials nearby are near 40 percent with a check-in rate of over 7 percent, that translates into a new "feet in the door" metric.

Keep in mind that the number of unique check-ins helps determine the number of customers checking in because some customers will check in multiple times over the course of a day or week.

Also be sure to track the following:

- **Mayor/leader turnover:** High turnover is actually a good thing because it means that people are vying to be the top "checker-inner" at your venue.

- **Demographic breakdown:** This should match with your target customer profile.

Not all of these KPIs will be applicable to your campaign. For instance, if you're running a marketing campaign for a software company, the number of photos posted might not be of significance. If you're running a marketing campaign for a restaurant, however, you'll probably place a premium on the number of people taking pictures of your food and sharing them.

If you think of the overarching KPI that your business can focus on, you can start to align the right location-based KPI with your campaign. Here are the four different types of KPI:

- **Net increase in month-over-month sales:** Increasing check-ins can increase sales.

- **Customer satisfaction, as measured by Net Promoter Score (NPS):** This is a widely used methodology where you subtract your net detractors from your net promoters. This is based on the question of whether a customer would recommend your company's products and/or services to friends and family. To find out more about NPS, go to www.netpromoter.com.

- **Spending per customer per visit:** Your goal is to encourage existing customers to give you a greater share of their wallet on each visit.

- **Customer loyalty:** This is based on how many customers are repeat customers.

If you look at these four areas as follows, you can start to determine what location-based KPIs you should be looking at for each.

Increase in monthly net sales

Think about what would drive an increase in monthly sales — the number of check-ins could help increase this number. McDonald's increased its daily check-ins by 33.5 percent during a one-day test of giving out $5 to $10 gift cards. (See the spike in traffic in Figure 11-1.) *Note:* McDonald's ran this test in early 2010 when Foursquare had just under one million users.

If your goal is to increase monthly net sales, create your offers to tightly correlate to the number of check-ins. For example, the richer or more creative the offer, the more likely you are to increase check-ins and foot traffic.

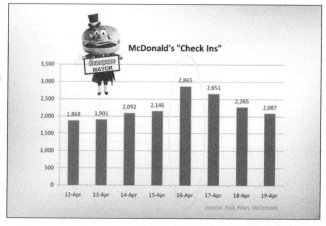

Figure 11-1:
Spike in McDonald's check-in traffic as a result of its foursquare campaign.

Courtesy of McDonald's

A second way you can increase net monthly sales is by creating offers that get better as people check in more. This could be as simple as increasing the percentage off the price of your merchandise or services. For instance, the discount could step up by 5 percent every time someone checks in, all the way up to 25 percent off, and then requires regular check-ins to maintain that percentage. Or the offer could improve with steady check-ins over time, such as number of check-ins per month, or you could even incorporate cross-venue check-ins, such as an offer of unlimited free drinks for a year to the participants who check into all eight locations of a particular restaurant chain.

Customer satisfaction

If your goal is to increase your customer satisfaction (your net promoters significantly outnumber your net detractors), you need to increase your customers' willingness to recommend your business. High touch offers can play a role here. Think about ways to surprise and delight your customers such as offering lunch with the owner/CEO or wine tasting with the chef or even an hour-long demo of your technology from the VP of engineering.

The KPIs you want to keep an eye on are number of promoters, number of detractors, and a steady increase in cross-posting of check-ins. Look for things like repeat check-ins and even sentiment where available (we talk about this a little bit in Chapter 12).

A key factor to customer satisfaction is making sure that you are operationally ready to deliver on your location-based marketing campaign. Even with the best offer, your customers are going to be hesitant to recommend your business if you make mistakes fulfilling your offer. Make sure you properly coordinate your marketing efforts with other staff members, so that campaigns run smoothly and customers are happy.

Also remember to reach out to your customers who regularly check in. Let them know that you know that they're checking in and that you appreciate their business.

Spending per customer visit

Getting your customers to come into your venue to buy something is a good thing. Encouraging them to buy more every time they come in is even better. This is traditionally called *increasing your share of wallet*. Sometimes it entails talking customers out of spending dollars at a competitor's business and encouraging them to spend it with you. (Starbucks did this when research showed that people weren't buying its pastries and food items, so the coffee chain began locally sourcing food items, which improved freshness and quality.)

You can also increase share of wallet by borrowing from other discretionary spending areas. For example, a grocery store might offer prepared meals that some customers might purchase in lieu of dining out — a cost-cutting measure for the customer and a revenue increase for the grocery store. Grocery stores could help steer this process by creating offers that are time sensitive. For example, anyone checking into the store after 6 PM gets a get a free prepared meal offer with any $20 purchase.

An easy way to increase the money spent during a customer visit is to upsell complementary items to customers. For examples, a stationary store can sell pen refills to anyone buying pens. You can use location-based marketing to suggest these types of purchase by leaving a tip or maybe uploading pictures of your pen refill section so that customers know that you have them.

You can also extend offers that most customers are likely to upsize. For example, a museum can offer a $5 item in the gift shop with a foursquare check-in and purchase of a full-priced ticket. Most likely customers will upsize the $5 item (buy a more expensive item) or buy an additional item.

Customer loyalty

Customer loyalty is one of the KPIs most easily impacted by location-based marketing. The beauty of loyalty as a KPI is that a loyal customer base helps many of your other KPIs, including satisfaction, sales, and share of wallet, because loyal customers tend to drive referrals, sales, and customer retention.

To get a gauge of how your business is doing on the loyalty front, you have to look at repeat check-ins, tips, pictures from repeat check-ins, and regular cross-posting on other social networks (particularly when there is positive sentiment).

When you create offers that apply to all of your customers or offers that get better over time, you're more likely to gain customer loyalty. They'll keep coming back to you to get additional offers that they're not getting at your competitor.

Driving deeper loyalty using reward services

A good example of a customer loyalty driver is the program shopkick (www.shopkick.com), which Best Buy (as well as other companies) has rolled out. If a customer walks into a Best Buy with the shopkick app open, she's automatically checked in and gains kickbucks. She can exchange her kickbucks for gift certificates, donations to nonprofits, and other items.

A customer can also scan items for additional kickbucks and specials. shopkick rewards work across multiple venues, so customers can earn dollars not just by checking into Best Buy but for checking in and scanning items in other stores, including Target, Sports Authority, and Simon Malls stores. This is good for Best Buy and the other participating stores because they're all essentially participating in one big loyalty program that's more fun and engaging than just a company-specific loyalty reward program.

Finding the Value of a Check-in

Location-based marketing really comes down to the check-in. If you can determine the value a check-in has for your business, you can determine how much you can afford to spend on an offer as well as marketing your program in general.

To measure your success, you need to compare the number of customers who have checked in with those who haven't. If you don't have an accurate way of tracking this, you can achieve this via a qualitative measure like a post-campaign customer survey. If you can tie a check-in to individual customer activity (see Chapter 5 on how to connect your LBS data to your CRM efforts), this comparison should be a relatively straightforward process.

Lifetime value of a customer is a great metric to measure, but that takes years to measure properly. In this section, we tackle two ways to measure your campaign in the short term: customer value and customer loyalty.

Check-in value

You won't be able to come up with an exact monetary value for a check-in, but you can create a value range for your customers. Follow these steps using your customer relational management (CRM) program:

1. **Run your campaign for one to three months.**

   You need to ensure you have enough data to collate. Allow at least one month; three months is even better. You should aim for 200 check-ins.

2. **Pull 200 customer check-ins (or a month's worth, whichever is greater) from your CRM.**

   If you have more, randomly select 200 of these customers along with their accompanying sales data.

3. **Pull an equal number of customers from your CRM who have not checked in.**

   Ideally, this group of people roughly matches the high-level demographics of your customers who have checked in. In particular, match the male/female split and age range.

4. **Compare the average amount of money spent per customers who have checked in versus those that haven't during that time.**

5. **Subtract the amount of money you spent on your offer from your gross sales from the 200 customers that checked in to get the average spent.**

For instance, if you make $10,000 in gross sales but spent $250 on offers, subtract that amount of money. If you spent any incremental money on marketing or any other operational costs like hiring someone to manage your location-based marketing program, subtract that amount of money from the net as well.

6. **Compare the average spent per customer to the non–check-ins average spent per customer.**

   Ideally, the amount of money that non–check-in customers spent on average is less than the number for those checking in.

7. **Subtract the amount of the check-in customer from the non–check-in customer.**

   Now you have the value of a check-in. Assuming the net sales for the non–check-ins averages $40/customer and the net average value for those checking in is $48.75, the value of your check-in would be $8.75/customer.

If the average value of the users who don't check in comes out higher than the average value of those who do check in, you shouldn't despair. You may need to allow more time to elapse before measuring the value. You can also look at other metrics, including lifetime value, loyalty (see the next section), and number of referrals (word of mouth) to determine value.

Net Promoter Score

Bain Consultant, Fred Reichheld, introduced Net Promoter Score (NPS) in 2003. With NPS, you can get a meaningful snapshot of your current level of customer satisfaction as part of a greater measure of customer loyalty. It stood to reason that if you have a high customer satisfaction, your company would naturally grow faster because satisfied customers tell other satisfied customers about a product or service thus creating buzz or word-of-mouth marketing. The most controversial aspect of Reichheld's construct was that you only needed to ask one question of your customers, namely, "How likely is it that you would recommend our company to a friend or colleague?"

To determine a meaningful answer to that question, you have to group the responses of your customers into three groups. Customers are grouped into either, Promoters (those who rate their likelihood a 9 or 10), Passives, (those that rate their likelihood a 7 or 8), and Detractors (those that rate their likelihood a 0-6). The net score is determined by subtracting the percentage of customers who are "Promoters" and subtract the percentage of customers who are "Detractors." The resulting number is your Net Promoter Score.

Always follow up on with an open-ended question of "why." These answers allow you to get a qualitative sense of why customers would or wouldn't recommend your business so that you can do more of what is working and fix what isn't working.

Customer loyalty

If you use Net Promoter Score (NPS), you can measure your check-in effectiveness as you would any of your other programs. Follow these steps to calculate customer loyalty:

1. **Collect at least 200 check-ins.**

2. **Pull data for another 200 customers that haven't checked in.**

   Try to match the demographics at least on sex and age if this is possible with your 200 check-ins.

3. **Survey both sets of customers.**

   Because loyalty is a little more difficult to calculate than something like net sales or share of wallet, you need to take a more qualitative approach to measuring. This is where the survey comes in. The goal is to get a sense of what the customer's mindset is and whether your program is successful. These type of questions determine whether the customer is already an advocate and whether they are using LBS:

   • Would you recommend Company ABC to one of your friends, neighbors, family members or co-workers?

   • Have you ever used an LBS to check into a business?

   • Have you ever used an LBS to check into Company ABC?

   Figure 11-2 shows a sample survey.

   Always include a "why or why not" box when you ask whether your customers would recommend you. Not every customer will answer this question but for those that do, you can get a better sense of why they would or wouldn't recommend your business.

4. **Tabulate your responses in a spreadsheet.**

5. **From the number of customers who would recommend your business, subtract the number of customers who would not.**

   This number is essentially your "net promoter score," although you should note that the official NPS is a formal measurement; this is only an approximation.

6. **Compare your net promoter score for the population of customers who have checked in to that of the customers who have not checked in.**

   Ideally, your net promoter score for those checking in is greater than those not checking in. If it isn't, you still have some work to do.

Sample Survey Questions for Measuring the Impact of a check-in on Loyalty

- Have you ever purchased something from *Company ABC*?

- Would you consider yourself a customer of *Company ABC*?

- Would you recommend *Company ABC* to one of your friends, neighbors, family members or co-workers?

- Have you ever used a location based service like Yelp, foursquare or Facebook Places to check-in to a business?

- Have you ever used a location based service like Yelp, foursquare or Facebook Places to check-in to *Company ABC*?

Figure 11-2: A survey to test whether your location-based campaign is improving customer loyalty.

Don't forget to look at any comments that customers left in your freeform responses. In particular, for those customers who wouldn't recommend your business, you will want to find out why.

Tying Check-ins to Sales

There are ways to directly connect your check-ins to sales, such as feeding your location-based data directly into your CRM system, but if that becomes too much of a challenge, there are other ways, such as spot surveying your customers post sales to ask if they checked-in, that don't require the A/B testing marketing technique we discuss in Chapter 6. Spot surveying won't give you an exact number but it does give you a good idea as to which of your customers are checking in and what the sales totals are.

To tie your campaign to a boost in sales, you have to take pre-campaign and post-campaign snapshots of your foot traffic.

If you can demonstrate a post-launch lift in traffic, and you know what an average customer spends, you can start to make an explicit connection to sales. There may be other external factors involved, so data here will be more directional than concrete. But it will give you an indication of whether your efforts are paying off — even if it's slow.

If you don't have a CRM system that measures the impact of an LBS campaign on sales or the ability to do A/B testing, consider qualitative analysis. This is a fancy way of saying, "survey your customers and ask them if the LBS campaign made an impact." While this isn't the most accurate way of finding out how effective your campaign is, it should give you an idea of whether your campaign is a success. Hand out surveys in your store, hand out postcards with links to a survey (companies like Survey Monkey offer free online surveys) or e-mail your customer base.

AT&T pilots SCVNGR rewards program

AT&T launched a regional pilot across 50 stores in the Midwest that leveraged LBS provider SCVNGR's rewards platform to engage customers in-store by asking them to perform a variety of fun activities. Executive director of digital and social media Chris Baccus says that AT&T was careful not to limit the engagement to phone activations, as many customers visit stores to buy peripherals versus new phones. AT&T awarded the following to participants who checked in and completed the challenges, with the reward based on the number of points they accrued through the SCVNGR games: a gift card for ringtone purchases, a 20 percent discount off the price of an accessory of the participant's choice, or $50 off the price of a Sound ID 510 headset.

In particular, the KPIs that AT&T was able to track with this campaign were sales and media impressions. Not all campaigns are this clear cut with such direct outcomes, but AT&T did a great job of setting up the campaign to measure lift and media impressions.

During the campaign, AT&T saw the following results:

- ✔ Of all the Sound ID headset sales in September 2010, 9.7 percent of purchasers used a SCVNGR discount.

- ✔ The company achieved local and national media impressions totaling over 23.7 million. (This is the earned media portion of LBS that we talk about in Chapter 8.)

- ✔ The sales results on the Sound ID 510 headset went from 95 per month to 205 per month, an increase of 115 percent. *Note:* There was also another incentive that ran during this period, so it's hard to isolate the pure increase in sales to the SCVNGR event. But it certainly contributed to the increase.

Chapter 12

Pulling Data from Your LBS Dashboards

In This Chapter

▶ Defining a dashboard

▶ Looking at individual elements within LBS dashboards

▶ Checking out third-party LBS dashboards

*Y*ou may have made it through your career without ever having looked at a dashboard. Lucky you! That shouldn't stop you from looking at your location-based marketing data in a dashboard for two reasons.

✔ Having a regular snapshot of your day-to-day campaign activity is critical in understanding how your campaign is doing.

✔ Seeing your data aggregated in one place can often lead to insights you wouldn't normally get if you were looking at it in a silo.

A *dashboard* is a snapshot of the activity generated by a particular campaign, program, or ongoing set of regularly occurring marketing efforts.

In this chapter, we show you how to use the dashboards that come with the location-based service you're working with. If you find those dashboards a bit lacking — say you'd like to have one integrated dashboard for all your services — we also show you some third-party dashboards.

One of the risks of using a dashboard is that you can obsess about the results so much that you end up spending all of your time looking at your dashboard. Being intimate with numbers that are critical to your job or business is rarely a bad thing, but putting too much effort studying the numbers can take you away from the most important part of your job — marketing.

Looking at LBS Data Categories

The goals and key performance indicators you evaluate your program against drive which elements of the dashboard you pay closest attention to. For instance, if you're looking to drive engagement, you want to keep an eye on repeat visitors and how much they're sharing their check-ins across other social networks and activity. That doesn't mean you should ignore whether they're taking advantage of offers (obviously that's a part of engaging them as well) or time of day/day of week, but those elements are less relevant to your engagement metric.

If you're interested in sales, you'll want to correlate check-ins with your offer take rate and cross-tabulate that with your overall sales. If you want to look at the connection between time of day check-ins and share of wallet, you would add time into the mix, and so on.

Not all of the location-based service providers offer dashboards. That is likely to change soon as more and more businesses start using LBSs. Of all the major players, only Gowalla doesn't have a dashboard.

For all of the different services that do have dashboards, the easiest way to access them is to log in to your account, and you'll be presented with the option of accessing your dashboard.

 Viewing your dashboard is best done via the web, either with a desktop, laptop, or tablet. It's hard to see the data on the small screen of a phone, and some of the dashboards are created in Flash, which isn't compatible with any of the Apple devices.

Figure 12-1 shows foursquare's basic analytics dashboard, which shows recent check-ins, time of day/day of week activity, and top visitors, along with most recent check-ins.

In general, the data from the dashboards fall into six different categories.

Visitor activity

In this book, we talk about not only the importance of understanding how many visitors you get but also knowing who those visitors are. Key indicators to look for here include

- ✔ Top visitors
- ✔ Recent check-ins
- ✔ Unique check-ins

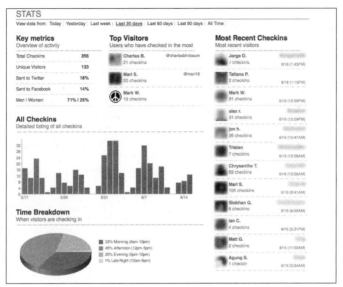

Figure 12-1: foursquare's business analytics dashboard.

Demographics

Part and parcel with visitor activity is demographics. If you think about the visitor activity category as counting "how many," think of demographics as data that help you get a better sense of important customer characteristics such as

- ✔ Sex
- ✔ Age
- ✔ Experience level

There's a good chance that your demographics will skew heavily male, as men tend to outnumber women on location-based services by at least 2:1. However, that doesn't mean that you can't try to tip the balance, especially if your customers tend to be predominantly female. In fact, this can be a great metric to pay attention to if you're interested in running some A/B tests to increase the number of women checking in.

Offers

By now, you know how important offers are when it comes to creating a successful LBS program. To that end, some of the most important metrics to keep your eye on are things like

✔ Offers viewed

✔ Take rate

✔ Number presented

Sharing

If offers are one of the most important metrics to keep an eye on to determine the health of your location-based program, tracking how frequently customers are sharing to other networks is probably second in importance. Key items to watch here are

✔ Cross-posts to Facebook

✔ Cross-posts to Twitter

Add your Twitter handle on your venue page so you can thank your visitors who push their check-in to Twitter. Also think about encouraging customers to use a hashtag as part of a contest.

When it comes to sharing, there are a few different things to keep your eye on in your dashboard:

✔ **Customers share on one social network more than another.**

It's okay if they are, but if that ends up being the case, that may change how you monitor — and how you respond.

✔ **Watch for drop off in sharing over time.**

This may be caused by offer fatigue or a decline in new customers. Sometimes, regular customers tire of sharing their check-ins for fear of annoying their networks.

✔ **Test to see whether certain offers or marketing tactics create a change in your sharing metrics — positive or negative.**

These could be signs on the door or posters on the wall. Turn to Chapter 16 for more promotion ideas.

Try testing tactics that encourage customers to cross-post their check-ins by using signage, specific offers that reward this behavior, or even a contest for the longest thread generated by a check-in at your location (with a screenshot of the conversation as proof). If you find that some of these tactics are working, your shares, so to speak, should go up. If you aren't moving the needle, consider holding an informal focus group with 10–15 of your top visitors. You can either @reply message them on Twitter and ask them to come in for coffee at a set time or put up a sign-up sheet in your venue.

Time

For some businesses, the time when customers are most active may not mean a lot, but if you're a retailer, seeing peaks and valleys in check-in activity offers an opportunity to leverage your LBS to drive more traffic during the valleys. In this case, important metrics include

✔ Time of day

✔ Day of week

If your check-in data shows peaks and valleys, it's critical to understand exactly when people check-in. When you know that, you can fill those valleys with specials, badges, or virtual goods that are only good during non-peak hours. This is the equivalent of a happy hour for bars and restaurants. The foursquare dashboard includes a Time Breakdown chart that shows when users check in to your location; refer to Figure 12-1.

Depending on your marketing activities, you can also make assumptions on the effectiveness of your efforts. For instance, if you run an ad in the local paper and see a change in the volume of earlier check-ins, you may have causality. Or if you put your table tents out only in the evening and see an increase in check-ins during that same time, that also might be correlated.

Activity

While many businesses that are using location-based services have yet to focus on the activity area, this could become one of the most critical areas of your location-based marketing program to drive. Just like with Yelp, numerous reviews — and in some cases, tips and photos — are a good sign of a healthy business. Data points to watch here are

✔ Tips shared

✔ Photos uploaded

Check-ins over time

You can also look at check-in volume over time; Figure 12-2 shows how the Yelp dashboard displays this statistic.

This is arguably one of your greatest indicators when it comes to the health of your location-based marketing efforts. You'll see a natural ebb and flow, and it's also normal to expect seasonality in your numbers — for example, fewer check-ins during the summer, more in the spring and fall — depending on your business.

If you see small changes to your time of day databased on offer activity, you notice an impact in your check-ins over time if you have dialed up your marketing efforts and launched a new offer, badge, or virtual good. Paid and earned media can also noticeably impact these numbers. Pay close attention to changes over time and do your best to keep track of correlations in offer, program, and marketing changes.

Printing your aggregate check-ins over time and keeping notes on these hard copies as offers, program details, and marketing tactics changes can be a great way to track success.

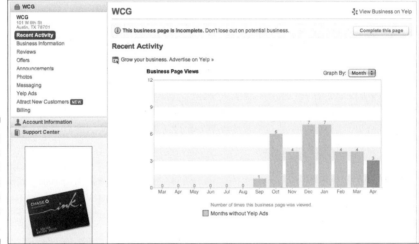

Figure 12-2:
Yelp's dashboard includes aggregate check-ins by date.

Your influencers

We talk a lot in this book about influencers; it's because they're the lifeblood of your program. Fortunately, with the help of your dashboard, identifying these influencers is easy.

The former Whrrl dashboard (see Figure 12-3) showed the most frequent "checker-inners" identified. On most dashboards, you can also find Twitter and Facebook profiles.

Figure 12-3:
The Whrrl
dashboard
showed
influencers
in the top-
left corner.

As important as it is to thank your customers for checking in or leaving a great tip or picture, you also want to be careful not to come across as creepy. Leaving a decent amount of time for them to vacate your premises (unless you run a restaurant and want to surprise them with complimentary desserts or drinks) is usually a good idea. It's probably best to send a public @reply message to them on Twitter thanking them for stopping by.

One other way you start to use your influencer, or even recent check-in, data is to keep track of when certain customers tend to check in. You may need a spreadsheet to keep track of this data, especially if you plan on tracking more than one person (which makes it seem a lot less like stalking). Think about ways you or your staff can use this data next time one of your regulars checks in.

Choosing a Third-Party Dashboard

While the dashboard of each location-based service differs by platform, there isn't much you can do to change what the dashboards look like or the how the information is displayed.

If you find those dashboards inadequate for your purposes, you can look at your data using one of the several third-party data aggregators. These third-party services can be particularly helpful if you're using more than one LBS — and even more useful if your business has multiple venues and or offers. These services — while only in their early phases — provide richer graphs, charts, and heat maps to help paint a clearer picture of your location-based marketing activity. These third-party providers will also likely be better at integrating into customer relationship management databases like SalesForce.com.

In the following sections, we talk about four third-party services: MomentFeed, Geotoko, Valuevine, and GoodEatsFor.Me.

While most of the dashboards are good, they may not fit your business exactly the way you need. If you have any technical chops (or access to some), consider building your own dashboard. With some of the functionality that customer relationship management tools like Salesforce.com provide, you may be able to directly pull sales data into your dashboard for a complete picture of your location-based marketing program.

Geotoko

`http://geotoko.com`

Geotoko is one of the first services to offer both analytics and campaign management for location-based services.

Figure 12-4 shows the dashboard from Geotoko that rallies around a multi-platform offer. What is helpful in the case of Geotoko are enhanced features like heat maps that show check-in density on a map. You can also use services like Geotoko to manage offers by type, time, venue, and service — all from the dashboard.

As of the writing of this book, Geotoko's pricing starts at $149 per month for one campaign across five locations. Because most of Geotoko's clients are larger agencies who serve larger brands with multiple locations, some of those clients pay as much as $9,999 per month. For larger campaigns, Geotoko also charges a one-time setup fee, which starts around $5,000.

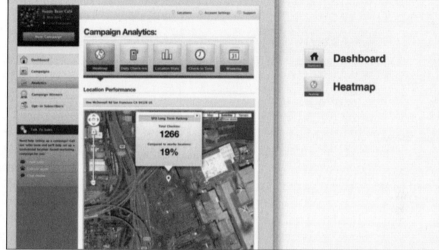

Figure 12-4: Geotoko shows heat map functionality.

Valuevine

http://valuevine.com

Founded in 2009, Valuevine helps retailers, franchises, and restaurant chains measure their location-based marketing efforts. In 2011, they launched a new platform that provided a much deeper dive into location-based analytics. This new product provides companies with multiple venues greater insights into customer experience, trends, and overall business health.

What's interesting about Valuevine is that it attempts to measure sentiment as well. As shown in Figure 12-5, the Valuevine dashboard shows Top, Bottom, and Most Changed sentiment. While this will be an important category over time, most providers don't measure it perfectly. Looking at changes in sentiment trends over time can be useful because the baseline is the same. However, it's important to look at some of the check-ins that are driving changes in sentiment — not just the data on the check-ins — because these can often be incorrectly swayed by sarcasm and occasionally, spam.

As this book went to press, Valuevine charged $299–599 per month for businesses with up to 500 locations. Larger businesses or businesses with greater needs can buy an enterprise license, the cost of which is calculated on a case by case basis.

Figure 12-5:
The dashboard from Valuevine measures sentiment across venues and platforms.

MomentFeed

    http://momentfeed.com

Created to help businesses with multiple venues monitor and measure their location-based marketing activity across multiple providers, MomentFeed is one of the first companies to offer these types of services. To date, MomentFeed tracks activity across 14 different location-based services.

MomentFeed has a little bit simpler interface than both Geotoko and Valuevine, but it allows you to monitor and measure more services and has powerful multivenue charting capabilities. As shown in Figure 12-6, there are at least 14 different services. MomentFeed also allows multiple users to manage one account, which is useful for multivenue businesses.

As of the writing of this book, MomentFeed charges $29 per year per location for their analytics package and $99 per year per location for access to strategy, CRM, and analytics. This pricing applies to only businesses with more than 100 venues. Pricing for businesses with less than 100 venues is a la carte.

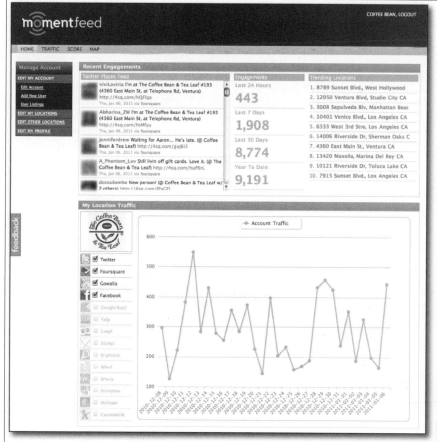

Figure 12-6:
You can integrate 14 different location-based services into one view with Moment-Feed.

GoodEatsFor.Me

http://goodeatsfor.me

GoodEatsFor.Me is a bit of a hybrid tool that is both a location-based measurement platform and a campaign management tool. As the name suggests, it focuses on the restaurant and hospitality industries. The platform provides these three different sets of functionality:

✔ **Reputation management:** Allows you to track your customers' conversations across multiple social channels including Facebook, Twitter, foursquare, Gowalla, and Foodspotting.

✔ **Customer analytics:** Permits tracking down to the customer and establishment levels across Twitter, Facebook, foursquare, or any other social network.

✔ **Real-time promotions and loyalty tools:** Facilitates targeted promotions to existing customers based on historical and self-inferred preference across social media channels. For instance, if you know you have excess burgers in inventory, you can offer a 25 percent discount on burgers to anyone who has previously checked in on a Tuesday evening and purchased a burger. With a few clicks, a promotion can be targeted to individuals who show an affinity for a certain type of food or drinks — across Facebook, Twitter, or foursquare — based on their previous activity.

The dashboard in Figure 12-7 demonstrates the richness of qualitative and quantitative data that companies can access when using GoodEatsFor.Me.

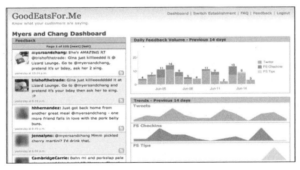

Figure 12-7:
Dashboard
from
restaurant
and entrain-
ment tool
GoodEats
For.Me.

Part V
The Part of Tens

The 5th Wave   By Rich Tennant

"For 30 years I've put a hat and coat on to make sales calls and I'm not changing now just because I'm doing it on the Web in my living room."

In this part . . .

We begin The Part of Tens with advice on the best ways to have a location-based service customized to fit your needs. We then give you our thoughts on what might be in store for the future of location-based marketing and tell you about some of the smaller and more specialized services to keep an eye on. The last chapter talks about ten additional ways to market your location-based campaign offline.

Chapter 13

Almost Ten Reasons to Start with an LBS

*W*e've seen a lot of great location-based applications and platforms created in the past few years. At this point, we have become advocates for building your application on top of an already existing platform instead of attempting to do something from scratch. This may seem counterintuitive to some companies who believe in building versus buying (or in this case, using for free) but in the early stages, we strongly advise the former versus the latter.

Here are our "almost" ten reasons why you might want to start with a product from an existing location-based service provider and work with that vendor to customize that product to fit your needs versus creating a platform from scratch.

Not Worrying about Maintenance and Scale

Building a location-based database is a hard thing to tackle on your own, so why not leverage a database that's already built for you? Platforms like four-square, Gowalla Places, SCVNGR (using Google Places), and SimpleGeo have already done the mapping, so you don't have to. Worrying about things like duplicate records, unified naming conventions, address standards, and accuracy is a business you most likely don't want to be in — and lucky for you, these platforms do. These efforts could be costly for you, and you would need to dedicate resources specifically to these efforts to be extremely effective.

SimpleGeo's API, shown in Figure 13-1, provides you with all the database access and documentation you could ask for.

Let the location-based service (the *vendor,* we sometimes say) worry about scale, which is one of those things that people with a good idea tend to think about later. If the idea is good — and romantic — sometimes people get caught up in the "do whatever it takes to get this thing up and running" mentality. Fortunately for you, companies spend time thinking about and dedicating serious resources to these matters.

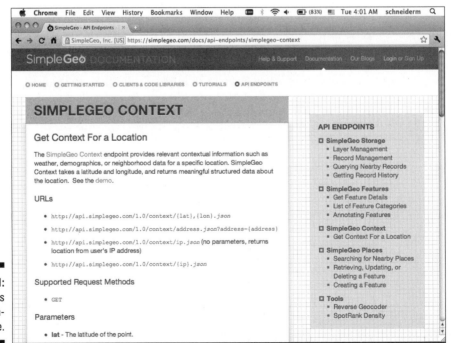

Figure 13-1: SimpleGeo's API is comprehensive.

Leveraging Base Functionality

With an LBS platform, methods and functions are already in place and ready for you to leverage via an application programming interface (API). Why rewrite the base functionality of checking in, friending and following, adding pictures, and so on when you can focus on enriching that functionality without having to create the whole thing from scratch? Basically, you can start with the platform's version of a function and piggyback your own functionality on top. Give this basic functionality to your designers and developers and allow them to be inspired.

The other benefit is that there will be functionality in the platform that you haven't thought of — often functionality that you can't see a need for now, but that you find useful later.

Integrating with Your Favorite Social Networks

When you're customizing an existing LBS platform, you might need to dedicate some time to learning about ways to connect your Twitter, Facebook, and other accounts to your application. However, you don't need to worry about writing code to get your location-based application to propagate messages via a check-in. Most of the location-based services already have that covered, and you just need to make it a part of your function call.

Remember that the people who use LBS (today) are largely a crowd of technology early-adopters. Their social networks are often vast, and they're a group of people who like to talk about what they like and don't like. Give them a way to spread the word beyond their LBS networks — but you don't have to reinvent the wheel to accomplish that.

Instagram is an application that lets you share photos with your friends. The app's developers integrated foursquare into their application after they developed a highly usable and fun application. The integration of foursquare has made their application even more appealing, as it will check a user in to a place and also push the photo into foursquare. In this case, foursquare is the larger network. The Foodspotting developers did the same with their application, which allows you to take pictures of dishes in restaurants so that people can pre-discover their lunches and dinners.

Even the Gowalla developers integrated foursquare into their application in order to show that they don't see themselves as a direct competitor to foursquare. Gowalla's API, shown in Figure 13-2, is clean and well-documented, making it easy for developers to use.

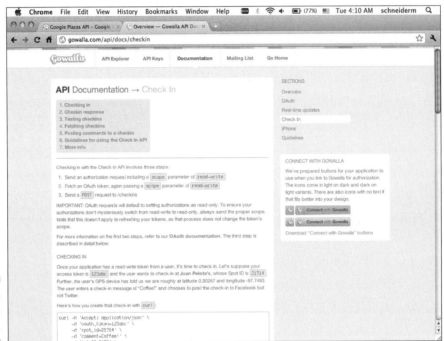

Figure 13-2:
Gowalla's
API.

Getting Extra Promotion

It's nice to be liked, and it's nice to get some love and attention from other companies. If you do something cool, the location-based service might start talking about it along with you. Partnering these days is more than signing a document and paying someone to do something. The people on the location-based service side care more about your success on their platform than just the money in the bank. In the age of listening, you'll find that if you do pay for a location-based service, particularly those in earlier stages, they become focused on you, and sometimes you even have the ability to affect change on the platform. In other words, location-based services listen and build features based on what the power users on both the consumer and business sides want.

Figure 13-3 shows how foursquare promotes third-party applications in its app gallery, giving them extra attention and earned media.

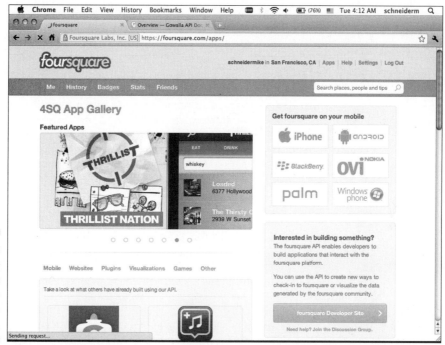

Figure 13-3:
foursquare
promotes
applications
in its app
gallery.

Alleviating the Technical Headaches

One of the problems with creating your own platform is that you're responsible for the maintenance and upkeep of your own platform. Using someone else's platform, especially when the platform is free, can save time, money, and headaches. For instance, think about how you might handle these scenarios:

- The system goes down.
- Users demand functionality that doesn't exist, maybe even a feature that a competing platform offers, and you don't currently have the resources to develop it.
- You find that you need a specific kind of data but don't know how to get it.

Yes, there can be advantages to controlling your own destiny, but unless your company has the resources and bandwidth to take on building its own platform, along with maintaining and updating that platform, we strongly suggest considering leaving the headaches to an existing location-based service provider.

Focusing on the Data

If your company is like most companies, it has limited technical resources. Unless your company is different, use those scarce resources to focus on extracting data from your location-based service of choice so that it can be captured in your own database. This way, you get the benefit of having all of the place data at your disposal without having to worry about making sure the platform is available. You can build data marts to capture the data that you would like to use for analysis, and you can put it in your CRM system to make sure that it goes away.

While many of the location-based services have the best intentions to create enterprise-grade dashboards and analytics tools, it's not usually their strong suit. Yes, they capture data and talk about what they will do once they get critical mass of data, but analytics and data visualization often aren't in their DNA, and the efforts in analysis are often weak.

The point we're making here is that you can take the data you collect and partner with a more focused location-based service. Even if you have the resources to build your own application from scratch, you might find, instead, that spending that money on building something on top of foursquare, Gowalla, Google Places, or SimpleGeo can prove much more effective.

Focusing on Your Own Business Goals

Remember those LBS-developer entrepre-nerds that we discuss earlier? Their business and livelihood is the check-in, capturing the data, (sometimes) the analytics, and the platform. Yours is selling a product or service. Your focus is on your business, not on developing products and services that complement your business. Letting someone else do the hard work of developing and maintaining these tools gives you the time to focus on what you do best.

Location-based services figure out the hard problems for you. They test whether people will use the platform and do something that you probably cannot do: recruit the best damn developers in the world and feed them copious amounts of Mountain Dew and burritos from places like Taqueria Cancun in San Francisco or Anna's Taqueria in Boston. The location-based service providers do things like unit testing and even play testing of concepts and will talk about their experiences with building the application and why they made the decisions that they made versus some that may have seemed like better ideas. The point is that they have already sat in boardrooms, restaurants, and coffee shops and hashed out big infrastructure and functionality ideas on iPads, whiteboards, moleskins, and latte-stained napkins.

Tapping into Cross-Industry Knowledge

Many companies chose to use ad agencies and third-party vendors even though they could theoretically hire the same talent and keep them all to themselves. In spite of all the money they could save by doing this, they still hire outside. Of course, one of the reasons is because this gives them flexibility, but another main reason companies do this is because they get the benefit of their agency partner's experience with other clients. In some cases, the other clients are within the same industry. Other times, they're outside the industry.

Where's the connection here? Using a location-based service provider that has benefited from working with multiple clients gives you access to innovation that you couldn't ever possibly gain on your own. So rather than spending your time figuring out how to keep up with the mainstream location-based providers' platforms, why not invest that same time in learning from what your competitors and others outside your industry are doing.

Chapter 14

Ten (Or More) Ways Location-Based Services Will Impact the Future of Marketing

To this point, we've focused on the point of maturity in the space and how you can get value out of the tools, applications, and platforms available. As a smart marketer, you also need to look to the future to keep abreast of developments that can help you get an advantage.

All Loyalty Becomes Social

The fact that people can voluntarily opt to tie their social profiles to a loyalty program opens a whole new world of segmentation to marketers. Personalization in the past has been based on high-level segments based on where people live and their family size, age, income, and job. With social loyalty, you enter a whole new world of nanosegmentation possibilities.

Imagine segments of people who like to tweet about their Zappos purchases, eat burritos, drink craft beer, and go to the park on Thursdays. That potential is here now, but very few companies are harnessing it across earned media channels. Companies like WHERE, Bizzy, foursquare, and Gowalla are building more sophisticated ways to allow you to target people using their check-in history. This potentially highly customized profiling will allow you to fundamentally change the way you talk to your customers. Imagine being able to say: I only want to target fans of indie rock who have an iPhone and have checked into at least three Starbucks.

We see a move toward segmenting customers based on interests, the places they go, and even the brands that they converse with. Combine this with location and purchase history and you have more information than ever to predict whether you will gain a profitable, loyal customer.

Knowing a Person's True Intent

In the current state, we still have to do a lot of guessing based on where a person has been, the kinds of conversations they are having, and the things they have bought in the past. Technologies that allow you to figure out when a person is going to do something before they do it are here. Applications like Plancast (`http://plancast.com`) and Ditto (`www.ditto.me`) allow you to see where a person intends to be; you can then tailor offers to them based on their proximity to decision point.

In Chapter 15, we talk more about each of these services.

Your Facebook Concierge

Facebook is collecting location data from foursquare, Gowalla, Yelp, Twitter, and more, collecting status updates, Likes, tweets, and blog posts, to name a few. Facebook also has some ways to get information on what users buy or intend to buy, particularly if they announce on Facebook that they bought something, via status update or (gasp) using Facebook Credits. This gives Facebook the richest information about users and could potentially allow them to become a concierge. People could even find information on Facebook instead of searching Google, telling Facebook that they want sushi, for instance, with Facebook making recommendations based on location or what friends like.

This is the future of paid search. Even though the recommendations come from friends, imagine being able to pay to have your brand's message high-lighted or prioritized in the resulting recommendations.

Coupons and Deals Feel like Recommendations and Content

Having context like location allows you to do things in such a way that makes deals that you send to people feel more like content than a deal or an ad. Content is something that a person welcomes and that they have asked for and opted in to receiving. Coupons and deals attempt to break through the clutter. They're intrusive and may not resonate with a customer's needs. Good content is relevant to a customer's purposes and nearly always what he needs when he needs it. Deals, offers, and coupons won't go away; they'll just be more highly targeted.

The Destruction of Serendipity

Recommendations are everywhere, from foursquare tips to Yelp reviews and Gowalla Highlights. Some technologies like WHERE and Bizzy are building recommendation engines based on behavior and giving a lot of assistance to the discovery aspect of exploration. The more you buy from Amazon.com, the more suggestions it makes for what you might want to buy next. This is because Amazon has incorporated a recommendation engine into its technology. Recommendation engines use information about customers to figure out things that they would like to do and then make suggestions.

WHERE is a recommendation engine that uses the things users have designated as favorites to make personal recommendations. Users can even bump phones with a friend to combine preferences and pick a perfect place. Bump is an application that literally allows a user to tap (bump) someone else's phone to exchange contact information. It even works across platforms. For instance, Android to iPhone.

WHERE has incorporated this into their technology. What's happening is that WHERE is looking at the preferences of both users and building a data set based on the "intersect" principle. This principle takes looks at both data sets and creates a new data set based on the commonalities.

Be sure to look into WHERE's capabilities around geofencing, which allows you to trigger offers when people enter a certain area you designate. You can feature your business in mobile search results based on keywords.

foursquare's explore feature is taking advantage of tips from users and businesses. When a user wants something, he can explore foursquare to see if it is nearby. For example, someone in New York City wants some gnudi. Searching for *gnudi downtown* might yield a tip attached to the Spotted Pig.

foursquare explore is a great way to get involved with geofencing if you don't have a brick-and-mortar business location.

Checking In Becomes Somewhat Passive

Eventually, no one will need to go to an app to check in; we'll even have many different ways for checking in.

Science has developed inexpensive sensors that use near field communication (NFC) technologies to send information to phones. This will allow a customer to touch a sensor on a phone to transfer data from one phone to another. Touching a menu item on a menu could tell you not only is a user at the Ninety Nine Restaurant in Charlestown, MA, but sitting at table 3 and would like the panko-encrusted Haddock. This process is lot less intrusive to the check-in flow because checking in can be incorporated into the experience, while doing something like ordering your food is the reason you came to the restaurant.

Technology will also allow check-ins with everyday, natural behaviors such as scanning credit cards with set preferences. Right now technologies only allow people to show exactly where they are by actively checking in, but current GPS and cell tower data alone is not quite precise enough to pinpoint whether someone is at the Puppy Palace or next door at Porndamonium. These technologies will help make that distinction (and save potential embarrassment).

Everything Is Semantic

Flexibility is the enemy of analysis. Checking in puts structure around the places that people go and makes it easier to pluck bits of information from the database and give you access to all of the additional information attached. Imagine that someone is interested in having a hamburger near University of Southern California. (Any Trojan fans reading? Tweet "Go Trojans" to @aaronstrout and @schneidermike.) He could tweet something like "Go to In and Out Burger. It's great." That's okay, but it still leaves a lot of unanswered questions like: Where is In and Out Burger? What should I eat there? How many people like it? What if you could tell your friend: "Go to In and Out Burger", but attach the place record on foursquare, Yelp, or Foodspotting? It's still a very short and sweet message, but friends now have a treasure trove of further information in tips, specials, reviews, directions from where he is, pictures of dishes, and more.

Tracking Is Social

Want to know where your trucks are? Want to find your employees? What about your shipments? Where are they right now? These types of tracking exist now, but what about opening them to the public? This technology will allow everyday people to track their deliveries and shipments and perhaps even foresee problems.

We talk more about services that use these technologies in Chapter 15.

Building a Game Layer

SCVNGR's aim is to build a game layer on top of the world. The game layer in SCNVGR's case consists of things that make the world more interesting, and it's an influence layer that encourages behavior from people and does it in a way that's fun. It employs several dynamics:

- ✔ **Appointment dynamic:** Requires participants to do something at a certain time. To win, a user simply shows up whenever they're supposed to show up (for example, during Happy Hour).

- ✔ **Influence and status:** Playing the game gives someone status. As levels go up, he earns achievements like badges that show status. The best example in real life? Gold or black credit cards.

- ✔ **Progression:** Think about the Legend of Zelda: As you gain experience, you get better items. You can't possibly defeat Gannon in the beginning — you need to gain skill, hearts and items like the silver arrow. SCVNGR works the same way.

- ✔ **Communal discovery:** Leverages the power of society to solve problems. The former location-based service Whrrl did this by allowing the community to vote on the best recommendations, determining who progresses and who gains status. SVNGR does this by encouraging people to play games and solve problems together.

Some people feel that these game dynamics employed in location-based systems go hand in hand with loyalty programs. Others think that they encourage exploration. When done properly and with proper support from paid media, these mechanics can certainly enhance the experience a user has at a location, providing the ideas are creative and you don't give users a big learning curve.

Personal Analytics Everywhere

Surfacing data that has been collected in interesting ways will keep consumers interested in using applications. For instance, an app might tell a user things like "this is the first time in four months that you've checked into an airport with Aaron Strout" — an interesting factoid. Look for applications like foursquare and Gowalla to increasingly provide people with more information about what they do and help them manage their lives better.

Web applications like futureme.org allow you to write a letter to your future self and have it sent to you in the future. Add location to that concept and you have 4squareand7yearsago, which is an application that tells someone where she checked in one year ago. It's fun to see if you're a creature of habit.

Give to Get

We're at the very beginning of an era, as data is now a kind of currency and will continue to be even more so in the future. The knowledge may seem rudimentary to you, but the data that someone drops everywhere are actually more like little gold nuggets to your business.

In other words, when someone provides data to your business you should pay her back.

Chapter 15

More Than Ten Smaller Location-Based Services

In This Chapter

▶ Ten niche location-based services

▶ Ten fun location-based services

Part of the fun and the difficulty of writing this book is that there are so many location-based services — two or three new ones pop up on a weekly basis — that it's hard to fit them all into this book. The fact that we don't feature them in earlier chapters, however, doesn't necessarily mean that we don't find them useful. In some cases, they're at too early a stage to know what their full potential is. Some services didn't quite fit the LBS mold, and then there were some services that we liked but found it hard to suggest for marketing purposes (which doesn't mean, by the way, that you won't find a use for them).

 Because the landscape of location-based services is ever-changing, we've created a wiki to keep track of these services. You can find all of the services we mention in this book as well as new ones at `http://wiki.locationbased marketingfordummies.com`. If you know of any services that we've missed, you can add them to the list.

Here are the location-based services that you should check out.

Ditto

```
www.ditto.me
```

Ditto's CEO describes it as "future foursquare." In other words, you announce your intention to do something. Users announce what they want to do and can find others who want to do the same — say drink coffee or watch a particular movie, as shown on the left in Figure 15-1. Ditto is even smart enough to pull in a list of all the local movies that are playing and then leave room for color commentary. Shown on the right in Figure 15-1, the user can type his intentions (or cravings in this case), and the app provides a link to suggested restaurants based on keywords in his post. The user can make the announcement public or private and, if it's public, cross-post to Twitter and Facebook.

Here's where this becomes really interesting from a marketing perspective: Ditto's technology is highly semantic, which means that it's particularly easy to tell exactly what someone intends. Unlike Twitter, where data is unstructured, it's easy to figure out the exact wants and needs of a user who has announced his need and location. If your business can service that need, you can act. The ability to interact with a person who you know wants exactly what you're providing is really exciting! It's then up to you as a marketer to provide the right offer to that person to see if you can get him to spend his time with your business.

You can make offers using this service to drive new revenue streams and fill in "valleys" in daily or weekly sales activity.

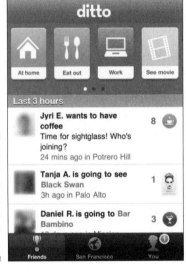

Figure 15-1: Jyri announces on Ditto that he wants to have seafood.

GetGlue

www.getglue.com

Instead of checking into physical locations, GetGlue allows someone to check into books, music, movies, television shows, video games, wine, celebrity gossip, and discussion topics including religion, politics, or history. The beauty of GetGlue is that it allows a poster to cross-post check-ins to Facebook and Twitter. This is particularly helpful to start a conversation about a movie or book, because GetGlue carries metadata about the media, along with a link.

Media apertures (preferences) is something that you've previously had to guess. But GetGlue can provide a very specific picture of a power user's preferences for reading, gaming, movies, TV, and more, as shown in Figure 15-2. One of the most interesting things you could do would be to use paid media to ask someone to check in to and follow you on GetGlue for a special offer. It's still early in its lifecycle. Early-stage startups are typically pretty flexible when they're trying to get users and businesses to interact with them. Take advantage of this by having conversations with them, telling them what you'd like to do and reminding them, particularly if you have a large media budget, how much value you're giving them.

Figure 15-2:
GetGlue shows a variety of activities to check in to.

Glympse

www.glympse.com

Did you ever wish you could send someone an e-mail or text message that says, "I'm right here," with a link to your specific location? With Glympse, that's possible. Even better, that person (or persons) can follow you as you move around for as long or short a period of time as you would like. And best yet, the people to whom you're sending your location don't need to be on Glympse.

The reason Glympse is particularly useful is that it's private (if you want it to be). From a business owner's perspective, it could be a great customer service tool. Think of being able to send directions to someone who is en route to your store, even providing a beacon to your exact location within the venue if it's a big-box retail store (or at a trade show if the layout of the showroom floor is less than clear). Also, when a person gives her friend or colleague a Glympse, she can often determine her desired destination. Imagine being privy to knowing exactly where your friend is and what route she's taking to her destination.

Here's how this app works. One user initiates the Glympse by opening the application and the Send Glympse screen, as shown on the left in Figure 15-3, addressing it using the contacts information stored on her smartphone, and selecting a destination, expected arrival time, and any additional comments. The recipient, who doesn't need to have the app installed, receives those details in a text message and can track the sender's progress, as shown on the right side of the figure. When the selected duration ends and/or the initiator arrives at her destination, tracking information is no longer available.

Figure 15-3:
Sylvia can send a Glympse to any contact and that person knows her exact location for the specified amount of time.

Instagram

www.instagr.am

If you like taking pictures and are active on the social web, you'll love Instagram. Equal parts Photoshop lite, so to speak, and a social syndication tool, Instagram lets someone seamlessly take pictures, add one of a dozen filters (many retro in style), and then cross-post to Twitter, Facebook, Flickr, foursquare (with an ability to check in to the location the picture is from), e-mail, Tumblr, and Posterous. Even Foodspotting and Instagram have integration points! Figure 15-4 shows some of the choices Instagram affords users when deciding where to post.

The other infectious aspect of Instagram is that it creates a community of people who like to take pictures — some good, some not — through its light commenting and "like" functionality. Many who use Instagram claim to spend hours editing and posting pictures and commenting on friends' handiwork.

Instagram has changed the way people share photos, through an innovative new design. Sharing photos is simple, and filtering by users and locations is a piece of cake, thanks to integration with foursquare. While previous photo-sharing applications like Hipstamatic offered a lot more in terms of effects, Instagram has been more popular and more viral due to its cool, easy, sharing model.

Figure 15-4:
Some of the posting choices Instagram affords users.

Foodspotting

www.foodspotting.com

Another niche location-based site, Foodspotting, focuses exclusively on — you guessed it — food. Foodspotting takes reviewing food (and taking pictures) down to the dish level versus keeping it about your restaurant. This allows your customers to "recommend [their] favorite dishes and see what others have recommended wherever [they] go,"" according to Foodspotting. This service is already getting some traction within the restaurant industry. Look for it to gain popularity, especially as foursquare continues to grow. In most social networks, you follow people. In Foodspotting, you can follow people, dishes, restaurants, and guides. It's really very forward thinking.

Foodspotting is integrated with the foursquare API, which makes it easy to integrate into your foursquare campaigns.

As a marketer, Foodspotting allows you to feature dishes in guides. You can talk to Foodspotting about creating your own guides so that when people spot dishes that are similar to yours, your guide can show in the postspotting screen. These guides give users collections of ideas from brands and critics. Users can even follow guides so that as new content is added, they're notified.

Everyone loves to eat. Everyone has an opinion. Every brand could have a guide for their area (see Figure 15-5). Some of the guides are event interactive.

Figure 15-5:
Food-
spotting
shows you
foods that
are close
to you.

Localmind

www.localmind.com

Ever decide not to go to a bar or restaurant because you thought it might be too crowded (or too empty)? Localmind takes the guesswork out of planning an evening at your favorite watering hole or eating establishment. The service pings someone at the location — irrespective of what service they use — and finds out what the local scene looks like.

As a marketer, you have a chance to be that person. Imagine you're an Apple Store representative and someone is trying to decide to buy an iPad 2. She pings the Apple Store and asks, "Hey, does anyone know if they have the iPad 2?" You have a chance to answer with "Hey, this is Jake at the Apple Store. We are out right now, but more on Thursday." Who knows what an anonymous user would say to the same question?

Neer

`www.neerlife.com`

Unlike many other location-based services, Neer starts with a need, namely, making someone's life less complicated. In particular, a person can do things like create location to do's, and Neer alerts that person when they're at the location. What's key about Neer is that it gets closer to the idea of *passive check-ins.*

Path

`www.path.com`

Path is a high-profile application that's starting to gain interest. It's based on a concept of intimacy. British anthropologist Robin Dunbar proposed that there is a limit to the number of people who others can be related to, socially, in their lives. This number isn't precise, but he supposed it was somewhere between 100 and 250. For sake of arguments and explanations, many people have agreed to use the number 150. The higher the number of people you can maintain social relationships with, the better your long-term memory, so the theory goes. Path limits each user to 50 friends, as that is supposed to be the next inner ring of Dunbar's theory. In essence, there are 50 people that you trust and that you would invite to a party. Because Path is supposed to be a more intimate way to share pictures and videos with people, you need to choose friends wisely, as you're cut off after 50 people on Path.

Essentially, it's another photo-sharing application. According to the website, Path bills itself as "the personal network." This means that it's a place to "be yourself and share life with close friends and family." In Figure 15-6, you can see the straightforward interface that allows photo uploading.

If you're promoting a brand on Path, you know that you're "competing" against only 49 other people for every user you connect with on Path. The nice thing is that when someone sees your message, you're informed because their face is attached to the output.

Figure 15-6:
Path's straight-forward interface allows the uploading of photos with simple tagging.

Zaarly

www.zaarly.com

Zaarly is an online marketplace that gives the buyer a lot of power. First, they express a need in a certain area and they tell the community what they are willing to spend. You can see the needs expressed and can decide whether you want to bid for the business. The user can pick which offer to accept and can pay without taking out a credit card.

Geoloqi

www.geoloqi.com

This service takes a bit of a different approach than most other applications. The developers combined the concept of geofencing with the concept of "future you." With Geoloqi, you can create location-triggered events that will remind you of things that you want to do or things that you need to do when you enter certain areas. For instance, let's say that you're having a conversation with your friend, Amber Case (coincidentally one of the founders or Geoloqi), and she tells you about a kind of pastry pocket called kolaches. You think this is the coolest thing ever, but she swears that the only place you should bother trying a kolache is in Houston, TX, where it originated — and you're both in Seattle. Luckily, you're going to Houston in June, but it's January — and how the heck are you going to remember your kolaches? Geoloqi is how!

Geoloqi has layers that provide functionality. One of these is called *geonotes,* which activate when you enter the area that triggers them. You can attach a geonote to the Houston airport so that when you land there in June, you're reminded about the kolaches.

The other great thing about Geoloqi is that it's extremely private. Nobody gets to see your location unless you allow them, and you can set up windows (time periods) for how long that location information is available — for as little as 10 minutes.

Geoloqi is also a platform. People can build layers to be incorporated into the application. Currently, you can use only geonotes and a layer called USGS Earthquakes, which tells you when Earthquakes happen, but the possibilities are as endless as the data streams available. For a brand? The most obvious would be to create a layer that lets someone know when you're near their business, but there are other cool things you could do to provide good content for people and enrich their experiences. For instance, if your brand is about kayaking, you could tag all of the best kayaking spots everywhere and notify people when they are near.

Ten More Location-Based Services

Because there are so many location-based applications, many of which have cropped up within only the last few months, we offer another ten location-based services that are worth keeping your eye on.

CarZar

www.thecarzar.com

Geared toward car enthusiasts, CarZar allows you to snap pictures of your favorite cars, share, comment, and earn badges. Obviously, this is a niche location-based service, but it serves a need in the auto industry.

CrowdBeacon

`www.crowdbeacon.com`

CrowdBeacon is a location-based mobile application with a lot going on. Not unlike Ditto, CrowdBeacon allows you to express what you want to do and gives people around you the opportunity to respond and help you find something that suits your preference. You start by choosing a category. The categories include Active Life, Arts & Entertainment, Beauty, Home Services, Local Services, Nightlife, Restaurants, Shopping, Mingle, and Deals.

This application is built on an interesting premise, but the user experience lacks polish. You could monitor CrowdBeacon for opportunities to provide an experience to a person at decision point. The people who use it are essentially letting on exactly what they want to do, so you have permission to align their experience with the request. If no one is available to answer a user's request, the user can leverage integrations with Yelp, foursquare, and others to get related reviews and tips. It is a good idea currently in need of a facelift.

Fwix

`www.fwix.com`

Fwix is a geobased search engine that combs the web to bring you a variety of information tied to places and points of interest. The nice thing about Fwix is that you can start at the top and drill down deeper. The layout looks a bit more like a social network (as shown in Figure 15-7) than a search engine. It's organized by content types and has several tabs to allow you to filter specific types of content:

- ✔ **News:** News from the web.

- ✔ **Events:** Nearby, upcoming happenings.

- ✔ **Photos**: Public, geotagged photos from SmugMug and Flickr. A little creepy. We saw some pictures of people's kids, and they probably don't know those photos are showing up on Fwix.

- ✔ **Updates:** Geotagged status updates on Twitter (mostly).

- ✔ **Places:** Fwix has created its own places database pages in partnership with Factual. The page has location information, hours, price (if it's a restaurant), and more, as shown in Figure 15-8. Content is curated from sites like Trip Advisor. Related status updates and check-ins are posted from Twitter and Gowalla.

- ✔ **Trends:** This shows the most popular keyword searches related to a location.

Figure 15-7:
Fwix pulls
geotagged
content for
Austin, TX.

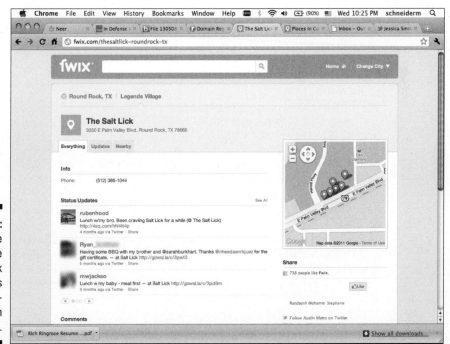

Figure 15-8:
Fwix place
page for the
Salt Lick
aggregates
check-
ins from
Twitter.

Advertisers have already gotten involved by featuring places within the results. Aside from being a search engine, it's also a platform, which means you can use the application programming interface (API) to build your own applications using its functionality. Its platform is currently free. The API allows you to filter places by popularity (which is related to the amount of content and check-ins attached to the place over a given period of time), and unlike some APIs, there currently is no rate limit, which means you can make as many calls to the API as you want. Many APIs limit the amount of data you can retrieve and the number of calls you can make in a given hour.

Forecast

`www.foreca.st`

From the makers of Hurricane Party, Forecast is a free mobile app that leverages foursquare's API and lets users share where they are going with their friends. This service has the potential to allow you to reach new customers by knowing who visits your venue along with those of your competitors. When a customer "forecasts" an intent to visit a competitor, you can provide offers to influence those potential customers. You also benefit from your customers broadcasting their intent to friends-and-family to visit your establishment. Forecast might be a way to have your most loyal customers serve as your social media marketing team.

44Doors

`www.44doors.com`

44Doors has taken a unique blend of technologies resulting in a creative twist on location-based engagement, launching its Capture platform that integrates short URLs, QR codes (a *QR code* is a type of bar code that smartphone apps can read), mobile landing pages, and analytics. As the first enterprise-level short URL service, 44Doors was early to recognize the needs of the enterprise for social media measurement.

A *short URL service* converts a normal, long URL (link to a web page) to a smaller URL that redirects to the original. This technology makes it easier to put long URLs with a lot of embedded variables and content into a post or printed marketing materials. For example, a short URL service called bitly converts this:

```
http://www.schneidermike.com/technology/ditto-could-
           unleash-the-power-of-semantic/1449/
```

into this:

```
http://bit.ly/dittofood
```

When QR codes came into the mainstream, 44Doors integrated its short URL service, allowing QR codes to be easily redirected to mobile-optimized experiences once they appear in print or online. Because the QR codes are encoded with short URLs, they render faster and are easier for scanners to read. 44Doors extended the solution further to include landing-page technology optimized for smartphones, tablets, and desktops. Instead of the typical QR code pointing to a nonoptimized website, Capture provides device-friendly landing pages that are easily updated to provide real-time, location-aware content. Capture includes GPS-based location information, allowing insight into zip code–level conversion analysis.

44Doors leverages SMS and short URLs in addition to QR codes to interact with the landing pages. Their focus on varying technologies as "doors" to their location-aware platform reveals a future path of expanding technologies that will likely grow to include new methods of interaction and location-savvy control of content. It will be interesting to see how companies begin to customize campaigns based on metadata such as time of day, network, device, and location. Companies like 44Doors that are investing in the intersection of time, network, device, and location and including analysis engines to determine faster paths to conversion will give marketers a true edge in location-based campaigns.

Groupon Now

```
www.groupon.com/now
```

Daily deals site Groupon has joined SCVNGR's LevelUp in the location-based daily deals game. This one has a bit of a twist. Groupon Now allows merchants to schedule deals whenever they want while also allowing them to expire. The idea is that they can create deals during times when they would not normally be able to get customers into their businesses. A person pulls out his phone, opens Groupon Now, and sees the deals around him in real time, along with how long the offer is available for purchase. The user can make the deal on his phone, and the merchant can scan the phone of the customer at point of sale to accept the transaction. This one has uber-potential for marketers, to say the least. Groupon Now is a quick hit for small businesses. Every business (in participating cities) with downtime can use this service.

Loqly

```
www.loqly.me
```

Similar to CrowdBeacon, Loqly helps you find relevant information by asking local experts. What differentiates this service from others is the metadata (or links, images, phone numbers, and so on) that Loqly sends along with its answers, making it easy to drill down into whatever it is you're looking for. One of the best things about Loqly is that you, the user, are notified as soon as someone answers your question.

RunKeeper

```
www.runkeeper.com
```

For any of the runners out there who carry their phone with them as their MP3 player, RunKeeper provides a real value by tracking your workouts. It keeps track of your pace and mileage and then allows you to make notes about how well your run went. Even better, RunKeeper allows you to cross-post your updates to Twitter and Facebook to let your friends know how your workouts are progressing.

Untappd

```
www.untappd.com
```

Untappd is one of several niche location-based services that focuses on beer enthusiasts. Beer services allow you to see what people are drinking and where they're enjoying those beers (see Figure 15-9). Untappd is integrated with foursquare, so when you check in to the beer you're drinking, you can also optionally check in to the place where you're drinking it. The app does all of the standard things, like pushing your check-ins to Facebook and Twitter. The potential to use this as a beer-finding tool is immense, particularly for craft beer, which isn't as widely distributed as the big brews due to limited quantity. We also see the potential for pubs to be able to push messages to its best customers when the beers on tap change.

If you own a brewery and distributor, you can use this information to determine which beers are popular. You can also work with Untappd to create special badges that users can unlock when they drink a beer or brand of beer a certain number of times.

waze

www.waze.com

Have you ever used a GPS navigation service? If so, the concept of waze should immediately become apparent to you. But instead of the navigation service just being trapped inside your car, waze comes with you anywhere you go, including on your bike or while you're walking to the local coffee shop. A key selling point of waze is that unlike other turn-by-turn applications, it's free. It is also full of cool user content. Users can alert other users to traffic issues, construction, police in the area, and so on. The one downside is that because waze is powered by users, it's only as good as the local network of people actively using it.

Chapter 16

Ten Ways to Promote Your LBS Program Offline

*J*ust because you're marketing online doesn't mean you can forget about promoting your program using traditional, offline tactics. While many of your customers may be online at some point in time, they may not be while they are in your venue — so remind them. And even those customers who are online in your store — even those who have checked in previously — may not remember to check in.

In this chapter, you'll find ten offline ways to create awareness of your location-based campaign, many of which are inexpensive and can be used in combination with one another.

In-Store Signage

One of the least expensive and most obvious ways to tell your customers that you're running a location-based marketing campaign is to tell them while they're in your store. This starts on your front door. Many location-based services even offer stickers for this very purpose. Figure 16-1 shows a SCVNGR sticker.

Figure 16-1:
A SCVNGR
sticker on
the door of
GameStop.

Consider putting posters or signs on your restroom walls, in your hallways, at the bar, in the lobby or waiting room, and even at your points of purchase.

When putting your signage together, consider using a quick response or *QR code* (a bar code that a customer can scan with a smartphone) to get people to your venue faster. If they aren't already signed up on your favorite service, they'll be prompted to do so. If they are signed up, you've made their journey toward checking in one step easier. Be sure your QR code enhances your customers experience and clearly explains what or where the code will take them. Most people won't scan a code if they think it's just a marketing ploy or fancy spam.

Here are a few additional tips when creating signage for your LBS programs:

✔ **Keep your message short and simple.**

Most people skim, so assume that they will read only a few bullet points.

✔ **Create a short URL.**

Use services like bitly (http://bit.ly) or BudURL (http://budurl.com). This makes URLs easier to type and provides additional tracking capabilities for you.

✔ **Include a visual element.**

If you don't mind updating your signage from time to time, consider including a picture of your mayor, leader, or duke/duchess on the board.

✔ **Include your current offer.**

If you're offering a special, remind people of what the special(s) is.

✔ **Tell your customers which service(s) you support.**

✔ **Remind people to add tips and photos to create a richer experience.**

Table Tents and Placards

If you own a restaurant or bar with tables, don't overlook promoting your LBS efforts on table tents and placards. Similar to signs, keep your table tents and placards short and sweet with only the minimal amount of information. Figure 16-2 shows a table tent at Golden Corral that encourages customers to check in on both foursquare and Gowalla and includes its current offer.

Table tents are a perfect opportunity to include a QR code that takes customers to your venue page. foursquare's Newbie Special allows you to give free stuff away as an incentive for signing up and checking into your venue.

Figure 16-2: A table tent at the Golden Corral restaurant chain encourages customers to check in to win an iPad or free meal.

Creating a short URL

Short URLs like those that bit.ly provides can be customized to make remembering them even easier. Think of something like *http://bit.ly/ EmersonsOnYelp* or *http://bit.ly/DocksideOn4sq.*

To shorten a URL, use a service like bitly (see the following figure). Create an account and then copy a link from your browser and paste it into the giant box at the top. To customize the link, click the Customize button next to the new, shortened link. You can make it whatever you want as long as it isn't already taken. Remember, though, short links are case sensitive — in other words: *bit.ly/Gowalla* is different from *bit.ly/gowalla.*

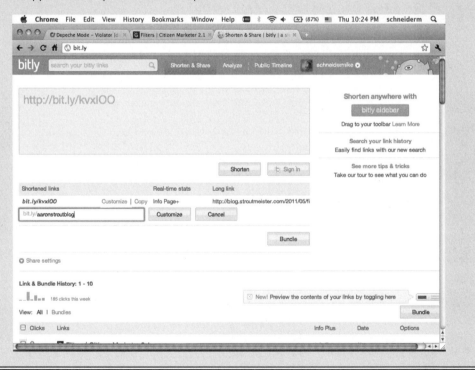

Staff Training

Be sure to train your staff to mention your location-based activities. Instead of asking about a special, they should ask customers if they have checked in. If they're unfamiliar with location-based services, staff can give them an explanatory sheet or spend two minutes to walk them through checking in.

This creates a lasting impression with your customers and helps deepen relationships. Every time that customer walks into your store and sees you or your staff, they will automatically think, "Oh, I need to check in." This is also a good way to make sure that your customers know how to check in and where to look for your specials.

Direct Mail

The trick with direct mail is to personalize it as much as possible, even including handwritten notes. If you're marketing for a larger organization with more than one location, this might be impossible, but for smaller businesses, this type of personal touch can create some real buzz.

If you've never sent direct mail, it's fairly straightforward. You really need three components in order to build your campaign:

✔ A list of the customers and prospects you want to mail (along with physical addresses, of course)

✔ Creativity, which in this case is a letter or handwritten note

✔ An offer and a call to action

If you're sending a lot of pieces of mail, you need some sort of mail merge program. (Try Microsoft Word.) If you're just doing handwritten notes, you can put your names and addresses in a spreadsheet. Figure 16-3 shows a sample direct mail letter.

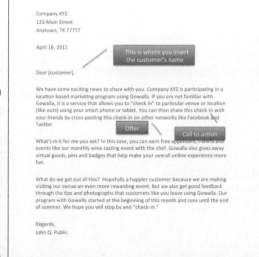

Figure 16-3: A sample letter with the offer and call to action for your location-based program.

Company XYZ
123 Main Street
Anytown, TX 77777

April 16, 2011

This is where you insert the customer's name

Dear [customer],

We have some exciting news to share with you. Company XYZ is participating in a location based marketing program using Gowalla. If you are not familiar with Gowalla, it is a service that allows you to "check in" to particular venue or location (like ours) using your smart phone or tablet. You can then share this check-in with your friends by cross-posting this check-in on other networks like Facebook and Twitter.

Offer

Call to action

What's in it for me you ask? In this case, you can earn free appetizers, t-shirts and events like our monthly wine tasting event with the chef. Gowalla also gives away virtual goods, pins and badges that help make your overall online experience more fun.

What do we get out of this? Hopefully a happier customer because we are making visiting our venue an even more rewarding event. But we also get good feedback through the tips and photographs that customers like you leave using Gowalla. Our program with Gowalla started at the beginning of this month and runs until the end of summer. We hope you will stop by and "check-in."

Regards,
John Q. Public

Outdoor Advertising

Outdoor advertising can be expensive — The New Jersey Nets recently spent almost $25,000 to advertise on the side of a building in midtown New York City — but you don't need the budget of the New Jersey Nets to have success with outdoor advertising.

If you have several stores or locations within a certain geography, outdoor advertising can be a great way to spread the word about your location-based services.

Most billboard/building owners can tell you approximately how many eyeballs your ad will be exposed to, based on car or foot traffic studies. Be sure to ask these questions before you sign any contracts.

When looking for locations to place ads, consider whether that audience can take action on your message. If you put your ad next to a busy highway, you may get a ton of eyeballs; people aren't in a position to get their smartphones out to follow up on your message. Try these places instead:

- A bus stop
- A subway or el line
- A local baseball field

Just like with in-store signage, include QR codes that allow prospective customers to easily get to your store's online venue(s).

Yellow Pages

The *Yellow Pages* is still a resource that many older or less technically savvy customers use. Including an ad that encourages customers to check in to your venue can separate you from your competition.

If your audience members are older or less technically oriented, this tactic can be successful if you use Yelp or Facebook Places, which have a broader audience.

At a minimum, include a short URL to get people to your venue. Include a reference to your offer(s) to entice people to check into your venue the next time they are there. You can also ask them to include their tips and photos.

Flyers

Flyers are quite effective for local businesses. The key here is making sure your flyer is well designed, clear, and correctly targeted. Placing flyers in the lobbies of local apartment buildings if your venue is downtown, or at a bus stop or around the local college campus can all be good uses of your time and effort.

If you know of other local businesses that are participating in a location-based marketing program, especially if they're leveraging the same platforms that you are, you can cross-post one another's flyers. Sometimes a strategically placed flyer on a neighborhood telephone pole (where legal) or signpost can not only alert customers to your location-based program but may even create a little neighborhood buzz.

In-Store Events

If one of your offers is a meet-and-greet type such as "lunch with the owner," or "wine tasting with the chef," that's a great opportunity to extend your marketing efforts.

What an in-store event can do — especially if you select the right customers or prospective customers — is better arm your advocates to tell your story. Because these kinds of events are fun and desirable, people should be clamoring to attend versus you having to coerce them into taking action.

Two things to remember when thinking about in-store get-togethers:

✔ **They don't have to cost a lot of money.**

In some cases, you might be able to keep this as simple as a box of donuts and a pot or two of coffee.

✔ **Target customers that have large social networks — on and offline.**

Some of your customers will be more influential and have larger networks — both in the real world and on the social web. Don't be afraid to take extra effort to ensure that these folks get invited.

Print Advertising

It's important to remember print advertising as a separate tactic. Print advertising includes your local or regional newspapers and programs for prominent sporting events or artistic performances or other special events.

Print advertising can range from a few dollars to thousands of dollars, but it's at its most effective when you can combine it with earned media. If you can get your local paper interested in running an article about your location-based marketing program and you can advertise with your own personalized message, it can have an exponential impact.

Just like in-store signage, outdoor advertising, table tents, and flyers, include a short URL and a QR code that can get your customers to your venue page faster. Also remember to include your offer and a definitive call to action, such as "check in to our location and get a free t-shirt."

Word of Mouth

Just like in-store events serve as offers and help drive influencer activity, so too can word-of-mouth marketing. The secret to making this work is giving your customers — particularly the ones that like to share — something to talk about. This is one of the reasons it's important to create great offers that are either easy to achieve or surprise and delight (or both).

While you can't really "buy" word-of-mouth marketing, you can create the right conditions for it to take place. This can happen in a few different ways, such as the following:

- ✔ **Video:** Create a video that talks about your LBS program and embed it in your blog, home page, Facebook Page, or even your venue page.

- ✔ **Activity:** Create a scavenger hunt or a contest where clues or activities involve or lead up to your program. Hide *Easter eggs* (things you find unexpectedly) at your venue, such as special pins, badges, virtual goods, or even specials.

When you give people a reason to talk, encouraging them to do so is the next step. Getting them to spread the word on the social web (YouTube, Facebook, Twitter, LinkedIn, and so on) are great. But a lot of word-of-mouth activity still happens in the offline world. Because some people don't have a memory for details, keeping your message extremely simple is critical. That means focusing on these three things:

- ✔ **A straightforward offer (something everyone can cash in on)**

- ✔ **A short URL that leads to either your venue page or a blog post that explains your program**

- ✔ **A reminder to check in next time participants are in your store (and maybe a reminder to leave a tip or take a picture)**

Appendix A

Technology Overview: Phones, Operating Systems, and Geofencing

. . . .

In This Appendix

▶ Pinpointing location on mobile devices

▶ Understanding location sharing

▶ Finding vendors who can provide location-based services

▶ Looking at the intricacies of operating systems

▶ Defining what geofencing can do for you

. . . .

*T*hroughout this book, we talk about marketing with location-based services as well as some tools and techniques to help you reach your marketing goals. You may find it helpful to understand how the technology behind location-based services works. As you dive into LBS, you may wonder things like how a device determines its owner's location and shares that with an app, how to determine which operating systems to focus on when developing a customized app, and you how can apply geofencing technology to your marketing efforts.

In this appendix, we show you the intimate details behind the technology used to enable location-based applications. We talk about what methods are being used today as well as emerging technologies in the space.

Calculating Location

Key to understanding how location is calculated on mobile devices is the concept of *triangulation,* which is identifying a location from spatial relationships to three or more key points. Based on a device's distance from nearby keypoints — whether they're cell towers, satellites, or Wi-Fi broadcasters — your mobile device can calculate its location.

When thinking about triangulation, it's helpful to think of keypoints as the center points on overlapping circles. Your mobile device can calculate the distance to each keypoint; it might find, for instance, that one keypoint is a mile away, a second keypoint is four-tenths of a mile away, and a third keypoint is seven-tenths of a mile away. There will be a small area that fits each of those criteria — that area is the overlap portion of the circles, and that's where your phone knows it's located.

In addition to triangulation, we tell you about three other methods: cell-tower triangulation, global positioning system (GPS) and Wi-Fi beacons.

Cell-tower triangulation

Most mobile devices have global positioning systems (GPS) to determine their location. The few devices (sometimes referred to as "feature phones" as opposed to "smartphones") not equipped with GPS can still pick up location and communicate it to applications using cell-tower triangulation.

Mobile phones are actually radios that send and receive signals from towers. As you move from one area to another, your mobile device receives signals from different towers. When your device receives a signal, it also receives data about the location of the towers transmitting that signal. If your mobile phone is using cell-tower triangulation, it's calculating its location based on the angles and distances of nearby cell towers and the strength of the signal.

Cell-tower triangulation can determine your location to within 400-1000 feet. This method is much less precise than GPS, but it's accurate enough for feature phone purposes, such as sending location data when making a 9-1-1 call.

GPS

A more accurate way of determining location is through satellite signals. Twenty-four satellites transmit positioning data. GPS works much the same way cell-tower triangulation does. Instead of devices positioning themselves based on their relation to cell towers, they're calculating location based on their relation to satellite signals. In the same way that you may lose your cellphone signal when you enter a wooded area or pass under a bridge, you will likely lose satellite reception when something interferes with the satellite signal.

GPS is very accurate and can predict a device's location within 10–50 feet. Often, GPS is given a boost of accuracy from WAAS (Wide Area Augmentation System) technology. WAAS is a collection of 25 ground stations throughout North America that collect and correct GPS data. When available, WAAS can boost GPS accuracy up to 500 percent.

Wi-Fi positioning

GPS and cell-tower triangulation work very well when you need driving directions, a list of nearby restaurants, when you're curious where your friends are, and much more. When it comes to determining location within a venue, however, 10–50 feet may not be accurate enough.

Wi-Fi broadcasters can predict a precise location within the confines of a venue. You may have seen high-powered wireless Internet broadcasters at conferences or events. In much the same way as cell-tower triangulation and GPS transmission work, mobile devices are capable of calculating their location based on how far away Wi-Fi broadcasters are and from what angle they're broadcasting Wi-Fi signals. With this technology, your device can calculate its location to within one to two feet.

Using Wi-Fi locating technology isn't as mainstream as GPS usage, mostly because application developers have largely focused on building apps that use GPS. If you're interested in leveraging the use of Wi-Fi beacons for your business, you can usually find developers familiar with the technology in any mobile application development vendor.

Audio signals

When we talk about audio signals in terms of location, it's using the sounds in a room to either position a phone or to decide if people are together. There are a couple of different ways to accomplish this.

✔ **Place a sound emission device in a set location that emits a unique sound.**

The emission of the device's unique sound, that may even be inaudible to the human ear, can be used to detect a device's location. The strength of the sound combined with the angle of the phone will let the phone know where it is in relation to the source of the sound.

Shopkick in particular is pioneering the use of unique, expected audio signals to calculate device location to within a few feet. Shopkick is a retail application that rewards users for, among other tasks, simply walking into different departments of a store. The application requires the retailer to install audio transmitters that send a constant sound undetectable to the human ear. Mobile devices can listen for the sound when shopkick is running and determine location based on the distance and angle from which the sound is coming.

✔ **Analyze the sound in the room and compare it to the sound of other people known to be in the same location.**

You need to use other location methods in harmony with audio signals, but it does allow the application to get a better picture of how close together people are by analyzing the similarities and strength of the sound. Color is an application that uses this technology.

NFC

Near field communication technology allows mobile devices to send and receive data over loop antennas within a distance of about four inches of an NFC receiver. NFC validates physical presence. Pinpointing a precise location sometimes requires interaction with something physical such as an NFC receiver. In location-based marketing, this technology helps to replace location (latitude and longitude) with place (a specific venue). So by validating which venue your customers are in, you can take the ensuing steps to further engage them. It allows for a secure connection that Wi-Fi may not provide.

Figure A-1 shows how near field communication technology works.

There are already several phones on the market that support NFC, including Google's Nexus S and two each from Samsung and Nokia. Apple's iPhone 5 is rumored to have NFC.

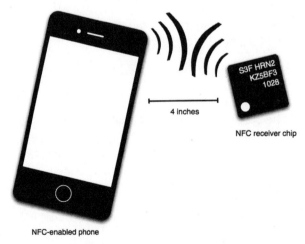

4 inches

S3F HRN2
KZ5BF3
1028

NFC receiver chip

Figure A-1:
Near field
communica-
tion.

NFC-enabled phone

Point of purchase

Points of purchase (stepping up to the register) can be used to determine a person's location for a short period of time. Registers are generally immobile and therefore allows you to pinpoint a user's location for a short amount of

time. The swipe of a credit card not only validates location, but can also provide a layer of interesting purchase data. If someone is using a loyalty card,
that person must be in that venue making a purchase.

The pioneers of social loyalty, Tasti D Lite, began experimenting with
making check-ins passive by linking foursquare accounts to points of purchase. When a customer makes a purchase, they can check in to the store
automatically. In early 2011, American Express began experimenting with
location-based check-ins triggered by credit card swipes. American Express
customers simply connect a foursquare account to an American Express
card, and when they make a purchase at a participating venue, a discount
is credited to the American Express account and they are automatically
checked in on foursquare. See Chapter 7 for an overview of social loyalty.

Sharing Location Data

To check in, a phone must first communicate its location to the application.
For that to happen, several transmissions occur. Here's what happens behind
the scenes:

1. Through JavaScript, the application requests the latitude and longitude
   of your location from your device.

   You can find the language of the JavaScript code in the SDK (standard
   development kit) of your device's operating system.

2. Your device retrieves that information through a mobile location provider (a server set up by your mobile carrier).

3. The mobile location provider communicates the information through
   the location-based API (application programming interface) to the
   server on which the location-based application is hosted.

4. The hosting server communicates with a content provider, which sends
   the content (images, maps, lists of nearby venues, and so on) back to
   your mobile device through the location-based application.

Figure A-2 shows how this process works.

Say you want to check into your favorite restaurant on foursquare. You arrive
at the restaurant and open the foursquare app on your smartphone. You select
the Places option to see a list of nearby venues. The JavaScript code within
foursquare requests your location from your smartphone. Your smartphone
finds its location through GPS and communicates the data to a server that tells
the foursquare servers to list venues around your latitude and longitude.

There are a lot of standard practices in place for protecting users. You need
to make sure your applications secure permission from users to receive

and transmit location data as frequently as their applications request it. Sometimes applications will request cached data from the last time the phone updated its location. Other times an application will request an update to the location data. Still other times an application will require constant location updating. These and other variables surrounding how your phone communicates location-based data are laid out in the parameters of the JavaScript within mobile applications.

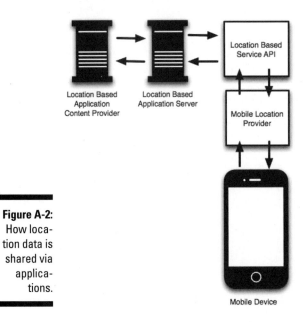

Figure A-2: How location data is shared via applications.

Developing Applications

Maybe the apps being offered right now don't work for your company or campaign. In that case, you'll need to look into developing your own custom mobile app.

The operating system(s) on which you choose to build your custom mobile app will depend on a number of factors, including your specific goals for the app, which audience you'd like to reach, and the development budget you're willing to commit to.

When building a custom application, you likely don't have to start from scratch. There are plenty of platforms with place databases and APIs for you to choose from, many of which are (currently) free. SimpleGeo, Fwix, Google Places, foursquare, Gowalla, Factual, SCVNGR are a few to consider. You can save users sign-up time by allowing them to log in with Facebook Connect or Twitter's OAUTH API.

Instead of building your own location database, consider using a platform to power your app.

Different studies always report different distribution numbers, but, in general, Apple's iOS holds the majority of activated smartphones, Google's Android platform is quickly gaining ground and expected to surpass Apple's iOS by the end of 2011, and Research In Motion's BlackBerry platform lags behind with a smaller market share, along with newly released Windows Phone 7.

iOS

Apple's iOS was originally built for the iPhone, but now runs on the iPod touch, iPad, and Apple TV. Apple pioneered the notion of the modern-day smartphone with the iPhone, and the iOS interface is arguably the most app-friendly of the available mobile operating systems.

Unique to Apple's iOS when it comes to location is the significant-change feature. Retrieving location information from a server can drain a device's battery. Apple has engineered a way to conserve battery life by combining cell-tower data with GPS. When you write applications for iOS, you choose from a number of options for retrieving location data. If exact location isn't essential to your application, you can program your app to request a device's location only if the device has travelled a *significant distance* since its last GPS update. Many times, the most recent piece of location data is sufficient to serve location-relevant content to a mobile device.

If the device begins to receive signals from different cell towers, it knows to update its location via GPS request, but if the device is still receiving signals from the same cell towers it used during its last GPS update, your app can use the previous update data.

BlackBerry

Research In Motion's BlackBerry platform is intensely popular for enterprise use, specializing in consolidation and streamlining of sending and receiving messages. When app-based computing models emerged and rapidly began dominating the smartphone space, the BlackBerry platform was faced with the difficult task of repositioning its established OS as a more app-friendly environment. RIM is still trying to complete that transition, and app development on the BlackBerry platform typically lags behind other operating systems.

The RIM Playbook tablet has Android app capability, so if your goal is the tablet market, consider making an Android tablet app, as they can run on Blackberry tablets as well. If the future of BlackBerry is compatibility with Android's operating system, Android apps might be a worthwhile investment.

Android

The biggest challenge facing Android developers is device fragmentation. Google developed Android to run on many different devices with service provided by various carriers, and that has created a challenge for developers who care about unified user experiences. Some Android phones have keyboards; others have only virtual keyboards. Different Android phones are running different versions of the Android software.

Developers like Android because it's extremely easy to build on, and the Android Market is unfiltered, which means that if you write an app, it's accepted in the market. Accessing location features through a custom application is a simple process on Android. Developers add a Location Manager feature that packages together functions for receiving location data.

Windows Phone 7

Microsoft brought Windows Phone 7 to the smartphone game late, but its development kit shows learning from previous players' mistakes. Microsoft is known for making development easy and efficient using their Visual Studio suite of development products. Accessing location features is very straightforward. A GeoCoordinateWatcher package documents a wide variety of actions capable with location technology.

Consumer adoption of the Windows Phone 7 had been a bit slow, but Windows Phone 7 brings a very different approach to mobile devices, claiming to be a quick-access solution to other operating systems. It's designed for consumers who want to quickly glance at their phones rather than commit to long application sessions.

While the user experience is slick, we caution against making Windows mobile the first platform you develop for, but do recommend taking a strong look at the platform if your audience demands an app.

HTML5

Many developers believe that the best solution to the crowded mobile operating system environment is to build web-based versions of the applications with interfaces that work on touchscreen devices (typically iOS, Android, BlackBerry, and Windows Phone 7) as well as on non-touchscreen devices (usually BlackBerry and some Android devices).

The introduction of HTML5 allows for excellent animation through the web browser bypassing technologies such as Flash, which is difficult to render on mobile devices (or impossible, in the case of Apple devices, which don't support Flash).

Mobile web browsers depend heavily on cell signals, which slows the process of mobile web browsing. Also, browsers haven't yet adopted native functions such as Bump technology and barcode scanning. Paging can also make the experience a bit clunkier, but some applications, such as Untappd.com, have done a fairly nice job of creating a clean experience.

Geofencing

Geofencing is the creation of virtual fences on physical locations so that when an activated mobile device crosses the threshold, an action occurs. Geofences are created by programming a perimeter into a geofence generator (establishing location) and adding an expression rule for that perimeter (associating an action with the location) into your application. Frequently, geofences are drawn as a perimeter around a central point, but they can also be drawn as polygons. Figure A-3 shows the concept of a geofence.

Figure A-3:
The geofence around New York University.

In the corporate world, geofences are often used to keep track of employees driving company vehicles or traveling within large defined areas. On a personal level, a geofence can alert you when your child arrives at school, via an application such as Neer. From an LBS point of view, applications such as foursquare use geofences to keep players honest; if a user is too far away from a venue (hasn't entered the geofenced area necessary for checking in), he won't be able to get points or mayorships for checking in. Additionally, you can use geofencing in your location-based marketing to deliver offers to customers at the most appropriate time.

Location-based ads

Mobile advertising has a huge potential for hyperlocal relevancy. Reaching consumers with your brand's message when they're physically near your venue is very powerful. McDonald's and NAVTEQ found incredible success testing location-based advertisements with a mobile ad that appeared on smartphone apps and the mobile web. Consumers responded with an astounding 7 percent click-through rate, and 39 percent of those consumers opted to be routed to the nearest McDonald's restaurant. Getting your customers off their couches, out their doors, and into your venues with television advertising is one thing; enticing them to walk into a nearby venue when they're already out in the world is another entirely.

Location-based couponing

Imagine walking down the street and getting a text message alerting you to a flash discount valid for only the next two hours. It's for a store that's only a couple of blocks away. You hurry over to the store to redeem your exclusive deal, feeling like a valued customer, proud of your own tech savvy.

That's exactly the convenience North Face offered its customers. In October 2010, North Face began its Summit Signals program, a service customers could sign up for by submitting their cellphone numbers. Doing so granted North Face permission to contact the customers with a special coupon or flash special whenever they crossed the threshold of a North Face store's geofence. The key to this campaign, and many other geofencing campaigns, is permission.

Fortunately and unfortunately, you can't simply blast cellphone messages to every consumer who walks within two blocks of your store. You have to acquire permission to send mobile messages, either by having customers opt in to a specific campaign or reaching out to customers in a customer database of previously submitted mobile numbers.

Placecast, a mobile marketing vendor specializing in geofencing, powered the North Face campaign.

Looking forward, geofencing should allow you to reach consumers at a point of intent, as opposed to simply a point of proximity. You can circumvent the assumption that a customer is ready to make a purchase simply because he or she is near a store. Imagine if North Face alerted its customers on the first cold night of winter in the region that it may be time for a new coat, offering a discount code at that very moment.

Appendix B

Getting Started with Location-Based Services: A Primer

In This Appendix

▶ Getting set up on an LBS

▶ Checking in

▶ Leaving tips and uploading photographs

▶ Understanding etiquette and the gaming elements

The primary focus of this book is to help you tap into the marketing power of location-based services. However, knowing how these services work and what the appeal is from a consumer's perspective will also help you better execute your own program.

In this appendix, we get you up to speed on how to use these services like a pro.

Setting Up Your Profile

Taking a little bit of time to set up your profile is a good idea, especially if you plan to connect with friends. If you envision using your location-based service more for personal activity than professional, consider sharing a little about yourself. If you want people to follow you for your restaurant tips, for example, let them know that you're a foodie. If you are a sports nut, don't be afraid to include your favorite teams' names.

If you plan to connect with only people you know well, you can allow your profile to be a little more esoteric. If you prefer to discover new connections or want to use your location-based service both personally and professionally, keeping your profile a little more straightforward will help you gain trust and access to those you want to connect with.

Choosing a Screen Name

Think a little outside the box when it comes to creating a screen name. If you plan to connect with people you don't know or use your account professionally, avoid names that might cause embarrassment or prevent other users from taking you seriously.

Most services limit the number of characters you can use, Get creative to come up with a screen name shorter than 15 characters.

Some of the services only show first names and first initial associated with check-ins, so if you are used to using a first initial, you might want to skip that and go with your full first name or use your middle name if that's what people normally call you.

Connecting with Friends

The topic of privacy, including who you should and shouldn't connect with when using location-based services, causes more debates than any other aspect of LBS. Some people are extreme believers that you should connect with only people you know and trust. Others love the discovery and serendipity of connecting with people they don't know.

There's no right answer beyond using your common sense. It goes a long way when it comes to who you connect with (and when you let those who you're connected with know where you're checking in).

Connecting Your LBS Account with Twitter and Facebook

Many of the location-based services encourage you to connect your account with Facebook right out of the gate. In some cases, the LBSs are offering this option to save you the trouble of having to reenter profile information (thus lowering the barrier to entry). They also realize that it will be easier for you to connect to friends, which makes using location-based services more enjoyable if you have an available social graph to leverage.

Most importantly, connecting to Facebook and similarly, Twitter, allows you to share your check-ins, tips, and badges with non-LBS users, making your location-based experience more relevant to a larger audience. It also puts you in the position to spread the word about their service to your friends.

With WHERE, you must connect your Facebook account, as shown in Figure B-1. WHERE likes to capitalize on the social aspect of its service.

Whether you should connect your Facebook profile to an LBS depends on the makeup of your Facebook friends. If you're close with the people you've connected with on Facebook, using your profile is a pretty safe bet. But will those friends appreciate seeing your check-ins, or will it become noise to them?

Any time you check in using an LBS, you always have the option to cross-post the check-in, assuming you've set up that capability, with Facebook and Twitter.

The biggest upside to connecting to an LBS using your Facebook profile is that you'll have an easier time connecting to other members. On the downside, if you plan to use your location-based service(s) for professional purposes and your Facebook account is primarily private, keeping the two separate is probably a good idea.

Figure B-1:
You have to download an app or connect on Facebook to get started with WHERE.

Uploading a Photo or Avatar

Some people are comfortable with putting a picture of themselves online; others aren't. In the world of social networking and location-based services, you should choose either a picture or avatar (or even a picture of your pet) instead of leaving the default account image. If you are setting up an account for your business, you will want to use a professional photo or even a logo to represent your business.

Consider these two reasons for using a photo or avatar:

✔ Adding a profile picture or image shows that you understand how social networking and location-based services work and are serious about using the service.

✔ It give others a quick, easy way to identify you and the information you submit. Some people use the presence of a profile image or the image itself to decide whether they should connect with you.

Signing Up for Foursquare

Checking in for the first time after you're set up on a location-based service can be equal parts intimidating and exciting. For the sake of simplicity, we walk you through this process using the popular location-based service foursquare.

If you're at your home, you might want to wait until you're somewhere you can check in to. The sign-up process segues into the check-in process.

1. **Go to** www.foursquare.com **on your computer or open the four-square app on your smartphone or tablet.**

   Figure B-2 shows the signup page in the app.

2. **On the website, click Join Now.**

Figure B-2: foursquare's setup screen.

You go to a page that asks if you want to sign up with Facebook or with an e-mail address. If you choose the former, you're presented with a series of screens — usually two or three — that ask if you want to give Facebook access to your account. For the purpose of these steps, we show you how to sign up for foursquare using your e-mail address (see Figure B-2; on the left is the web version; on the right is the app version). You can always connect your Facebook page to foursquare later.

3. **Fill in your first name, last name, phone (optional), e-mail address, password, gender (you must pick Male, Female, or I'd Rather not Say), birthday, and then upload or take a photo (optional).**

4. **(Optional) Read the Terms of Service agreement.**

5. **Click Join.**

   The next page (see Figure B-3) asks if you want to connect with friends. Location-based services are more fun when you're connected to people you know.

Figure B-3:
Add
friends on
foursquare.

6. **Decide how you want to connect with friends (or click Done to skip this step).**

   You have three choices:

   • *Scan my address book.* Have foursqare look at the e-mail addresses of the people you have in your default address book on your phone or computer. ***Note:*** It won't automatically pick these people but instead asks you which ones (if any) you want to connect with.

- *Find Twitter friends.* Authenticate your account with your Twitter account (if you have one). This also connects your foursquare account with your Twitter account for future cross-posting should you choose to go that route.

- *Find Facebook friends.* Authenticate your account with your Facebook account, and foursquare then suggests friends you are connected with who are also on foursquare. Similar to the Twitter option, this also keeps your foursquare and Facebook accounts connected in the event that you want to cross-post to Facebook in the future.

You can check one or all three if you like, You can also choose none and decide later.

The next step is checking in to a location for the first time, which we cover next.

Finding a venue

When you've set up your account, you can then check into a venue. (See Figure B-4.) There are other options at the bottom of the screen, but if you're just checking in, you can ignore them.

See your name at the bottom of the check-in screen? Click it to go to your foursquare home page, where you find your total number of check-ins, badges and mayorships earned, your point total, and the foursquare Leaderboard.

Figure B-4:
Check in to
a venue.

For your first check-in, a local coffee shop, restaurant, or even your place of work can be good first choices. Most should already have a venue established which will make your first check-in that much easier.

Follow these steps to check in on your smartphone or tablet.

1. **Touch the Check In button.**

   A list of nearby venues appears. (See Figure B-5.) If you can't find your venue, search for it in the search box at the top of the screen.

Figure B-5:
The foursquare app gives you a list of nearby venues.

2. **Touch the venue listing.**

   The venue information appears with an open text field where you can include some information (if you choose). This information is posted publicly on the venue's foursquare page.

3. **(Optional) Add details about your check-in and then tap the Leave Tip button.**

   Including color commentary on your check-in isn't required but is helpful if you decide to cross-post to one of the other social networks.

4. **(Optional) Add a photo.**

5. **Tap CHECK IN HERE.**

   We cover how to add photos and tips in the upcoming sections.

Leaving a tip

Leaving a tip is not only easy across most of the major location-based services, it's also appreciated by the businesses whose venues you're leaving them for. In most cases, tips are similar to virtual sticky notes that users can leave behind at venues they've checked into. They can be as simple as "Loved this place," or as complex as mini reviews.

You're free to leave positive or negative comments, but as someone that may be using a location-based service for their own marketing program, consider being constructive if you don't have something nice to say. Or if you like, you don't have to say anything at all!

A tip is additional commentary that accompanies your check-in. In the free-form text area, you have 140 characters to provide a tip — see Figure B-6. Sometimes, this might note a particular fact about the place, like "The food is great, but the service is slow. Make sure you leave extra time to eat." Or something like "At the Austin airport, the security line to the far right moves fastest after 10 AM."

Figure B-6:
Entering a tip on four-square is easy.

Adding a photo

The picture you choose at check-in can show your favorite meal, a staff member, or the landscaping around the venue. In some cases, photos at a venue can be gratuitous (which is perfectly fine). In others, they can provide visual clues on what to look for if the venue is hard to find or detail on something that's too complex to explain in 140 characters or less. The picture you upload is displayed on your profile page under the check-in. Friends can also see that you've just uploaded photos.

If you use a service like Foodspotting or Instagram, and upload a picture while cross-checking into foursquare, your picture is associated with the venue you're checking into on foursquare. Be careful about who appears in your photos — you may be giving them more exposure than they want. Photos can be easily picked up by Facebook and Google.

Looking for specials

Among the most rewarding aspects of participating in location-based services are the rewards and specials that businesses offer. Foursquare gives you the ability to see multiple venues' specials at a glance. This is good for both consumers like yourself and businesses, because if the special at one location isn't compelling enough, there are several others to vie for. And if many venues are putting out compelling specials, everybody wins.

You can find specials on the screen that lists nearby venues. (Refer to Figure B-5 to see that there are 13 specials in the area.) Touch the orange Specials button, and you get a full list of specials and their associated venues. (See Figure B-7.) As you scroll through the list, you can select whichever special looks interesting.

Figure B-7:
Many specials on foursquare and other location-based services need to be unlocked (activated) before you can use them.

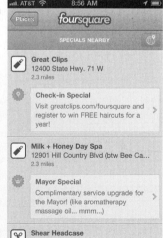

Sometimes, you must first "unlock" the special. In some instances, that's checking into the location. In others, it may require multiple check-ins or even becoming the mayor (the person who checks in most frequently over a duration of time) of the location.

To unlock the special, you'll likely need to show the screen promoting the special to one of the staff at the venue. (Figure B-7 shows what an offer looks like.) Because many business owners are still learning how location-based services work, be patient if they don't immediately know what you're talking about. As someone who's interested in using location-based marketing to promote a business, note how each business treats you — whether it's positive or negative — when you unlock a special.

Creating a venue

Depending on where you live and what service you use, you may not find your venue. While we cover how to set up a venue from a business perspective in Chapter 5, you can also set up a venue page for a location you aren't professionally associated with.

On foursquare, look for either a plus sign at the top of the venues screen or an Add This Venue option at the bottom of the screen.

Most of the major location-based services ask for the same basic information, which usually includes:

✔ Business/venue name

✔ Address (either through manual entry or by using your phone's or tablet's GPS functionality)

✔ Category (restaurant, printer, bar, and the like)

If you're the owner of the venue, you can also claim your venue. (See Chapter 4.)

Earning Badges, Pins, and Virtual Goods

While some people in the marketing, social media, and location-based services industries question the importance of the gaming elements, or "gamification," of LBS, we aren't in that camp. In fact, we're big advocates of location-based service providers promoting the gamification aspects of their services wherever possible.

Earning badges across various location-based services requires different criteria, but in general, you are usually awarded badges for meeting certain check-in criteria such as checking into five different Starbucks or several different airports over a specific period of time. In the case of virtual goods — something that Gowalla specializes in — there is very much a "surprise and delight" factor to this so you never know when you're going to earn a free taco, a first class seat, or a guitar amp.

Many people will claim that they don't care about winning virtual badges achieved for things like checking in to several different airports or Starbucks; however, the first time you earn a badge or a pin, it's hard not to get just a little bit excited.

Proper Etiquette

There are a few things to remember when it comes to etiquette on location-based services.

✔ **Limit your check-ins.**

Checking in too many times in one day can get obnoxious quickly, especially if you're cross-posting your check-ins into Twitter and Facebook.

✔ **Don't check in if you aren't there.**

You might also run the risk of becoming persona non grata with a business if you're checking into their venue but you aren't really there, especially if it appears that you're vying for a mayorship or another top honor or incentive.

✔ **Keep your private information private.**

Don't check in to your home, your kids' schools, athletic fields or gyms, or anywhere else that should remain private. You don't want to tip others off to your schedule.

✔ **Know who you're broadcasting information to.**

It's usually a good idea to know the people you are connecting with. You don't have to connect with everyone who asks, and don't be disappointed if not everyone accepts your invitation.

Beyond the Check-in

In this book, we talk a lot about the impact LBS has on loyalty. We would be remiss if we didn't mention the fact that using location-based services is a great way to discover new people, places, and things.

Discovery

If you've ever found yourself in a different city, new neighborhood, or even wandering around downtown looking for a new shop or restaurant, you've probably wished there was some way to find businesses that fit your need. You can always ask your friends via phone, e-mail, Facebook, and Twitter, but if you are in a hurry, that can take a while. Equally challenging is that if your friends or family don't know exactly where you are, recommending a shoe shop that is two miles away when you're on foot may not be as helpful as they thought.

With location-based services, you now have a way to start discovering people, places, and things that you're connected to (or maybe not connected to yet). Here's how you can find areas to explore with the different services:

- **foursquare:** Touch the Explore button. You can choose a category and radius for your search.
- **Gowalla:** Check out the various Trips people have set up of coffee shops, historical landmarks, and so on.
- **Bizzy and WHERE:** Rate past experiences so that you can find new ones that match.
- **Yelp:** Its augmented reality functionality called Monocle shows you in real time where restaurants are within your line of site. Even better, you can click the hovering restaurant name to get detailed reviews.

Another way you can use LBS for discovery is to search for like-minded people. If you love farmers' markets, try checking into your favorite one and see who else has checked in there. Or if you're a pizza aficionado, look at one of the local gourmet pizzerias.

Venue details

Have you ever been headed to a conference or a restaurant and realized that you don't know the address? Or maybe you know the address but wish you had a map of the location? One of the other benefits of LBSs is that they let you look at the venue details. Usually, those include a map of the location, a phone number, and the official address of the venue. Popular venues will have tips and photos as well. If you're trying a place for the first time, check out some of the tips before you go in. If it's a restaurant, there may be secret dishes on the menu. Or if it's a retailer, there might either be unpublished specials or racks that have hard-to-find specials.

Index

• *M* •

...e & Macs

...For Dummies
...0-470-58027-1

...ne For Dummies,
...Edition
...-0-470-87870-5

...Book For Dummies, 3rd
...ion
...-0-470-76918-8

...OS X Snow Leopard For
...mies
...-0-470-43543-4

...iness

...kkeeping For Dummies
...-0-7645-9848-7

...Interviews
...Dummies,
...Edition
...-0-470-17748-8

...sumes For Dummies,
...Edition
...-0-470-08037-5

...rting an
...line Business
...r Dummies,
...Edition
...8-0-470-60210-2

...ock Investing
...r Dummies,
...d Edition
...8-0-470-40114-9

...ccessful
...me Management
...r Dummies
...8-0-470-29034-7

Computer Hardware

BlackBerry
For Dummies,
4th Edition
978-0-470-60700-8

Computers For Seniors
For Dummies,
2nd Edition
978-0-470-53483-0

PCs For Dummies,
Windows
7 Edition
978-0-470-46542-4

Laptops For Dummies,
4th Edition
978-0-470-57829-2

Cooking & Entertaining

Cooking Basics
For Dummies,
3rd Edition
978-0-7645-7206-7

Wine For Dummies,
4th Edition
978-0-470-04579-4

Diet & Nutrition

Dieting For Dummies,
2nd Edition
978-0-7645-4149-0

Nutrition For Dummies,
4th Edition
978-0-471-79868-2

Weight Training
For Dummies,
3rd Edition
978-0-471-76845-6

Digital Photography

Digital SLR Cameras &
Photography For Dummies,
3rd Edition
978-0-470-46606-3

Photoshop Elements 8
For Dummies
978-0-470-52967-6

Gardening

Gardening Basics
For Dummies
978-0-470-03749-2

Organic Gardening
For Dummies,
2nd Edition
978-0-470-43067-5

Green/Sustainable

Raising Chickens
For Dummies
978-0-470-46544-8

Green Cleaning
For Dummies
978-0-470-39106-8

Health

Diabetes For Dummies,
3rd Edition
978-0-470-27086-8

Food Allergies
For Dummies
978-0-470-09584-3

Living Gluten-Free
For Dummies,
2nd Edition
978-0-470-58589-4

Hobbies/General

Chess For Dummies,
2nd Edition
978-0-7645-8404-6

Drawing
Cartoons & Comics
For Dummies
978-0-470-42683-8

Knitting For Dummies,
2nd Edition
978-0-470-28747-7

Organizing
For Dummies
978-0-7645-5300-4

Su Doku For Dummies
978-0-470-01892-7

Home Improvement

Home Maintenance
For Dummies,
2nd Edition
978-0-470-43063-7

Home Theater
For Dummies,
3rd Edition
978-0-470-41189-6

Living the
Country Lifestyle
All-in-One
For Dummies
978-0-470-43061-3

Solar Power Your Home
For Dummies,
2nd Edition
978-0-470-59678-4

Internet

Blogging For Dummies,
3rd Edition
978-0-470-61996-4

eBay For Dummies,
6th Edition
978-0-470-49741-8

Facebook For Dummies,
3rd Edition
978-0-470-87804-0

Web Marketing
For Dummies,
2nd Edition
978-0-470-37181-7

WordPress
For Dummies,
3rd Edition
978-0-470-59274-8

Language & Foreign Language

French For Dummies
978-0-7645-5193-2

Italian Phrases
For Dummies
978-0-7645-7203-6

Spanish For Dummies,
2nd Edition
978-0-470-87855-2

Spanish
For Dummies,
Audio Set
978-0-470-09585-0

Math & Science

Algebra I
For Dummies,
2nd Edition
978-0-470-55964-2

Biology For Dummies,
2nd Edition
978-0-470-59875-7

Calculus For Dummies
978-0-7645-2498-1

Chemistry For Dummies
978-0-7645-5430-8

Microsoft Office

Excel 2010 For Dummies
978-0-470-48953-6

Office 2010 All-in-One
For Dummies
978-0-470-49748-7

Office 2010 For Dummies,
Book + DVD Bundle
978-0-470-62698-6

Word 2010 For Dummies
978-0-470-48772-3

Music

Guitar For Dummies,
2nd Edition
978-0-7645-9904-0

iPod & iTunes For
Dummies, 8th Edition
978-0-470-87871-2

Piano Exercises
For Dummies
978-0-470-38765-8

Parenting & Education

Parenting For Dummies,
2nd Edition
978-0-7645-5418-6

Type 1 Diabetes
For Dummies
978-0-470-17811-9

Pets

Cats For Dummies,
2nd Edition
978-0-7645-5275-5

Dog Training For Dummies,
3rd Edition
978-0-470-60029-0

Puppies For Dummies,
2nd Edition
978-0-470-03717-1

Religion & Inspiration

The Bible For Dummies
978-0-7645-5296-0

Catholicism For Dummies
978-0-7645-5391-2

Women in the Bible
For Dummies
978-0-7645-8475-6

Self-Help & Relationship

Anger Management
For Dummies
978-0-470-03715-7

Overcoming Anxiety
For Dummies,
2nd Edition
978-0-470-57441-6

Sports

Baseball
For Dummies,
3rd Edition
978-0-7645-7537-2

Basketball
For Dummies,
2nd Edition
978-0-7645-5248-9

Golf For Dummies,
3rd Edition
978-0-471-76871-5

Web Development

Web Design
All-in-One
For Dummies
978-0-470-41796-6

Web Sites
Do-It-Yourself
For Dummies,
2nd Edition
978-0-470-56520-9

Windows 7

Windows 7
For Dummies
978-0-470-49743-2

Windows 7
For Dummies,
Book + DVD Bundle
978-0-470-52398-8

Windows 7 All-in-One
For Dummies
978-0-470-48763-1

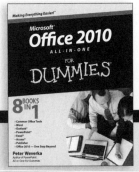

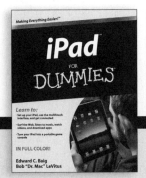

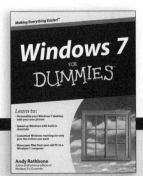

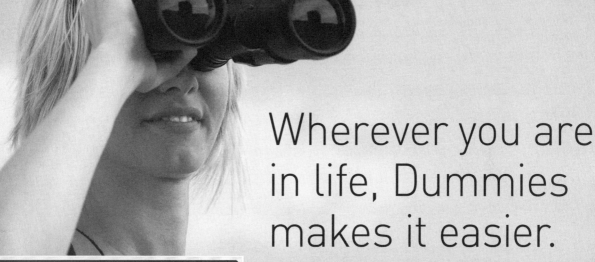

DUMMIES.COM®

Wherever you are in life, Dummies makes it easier.

From fashion to Facebook®,
wine to Windows®, and everything in between,
Dummies makes it easier.

Visit us at Dummies.com

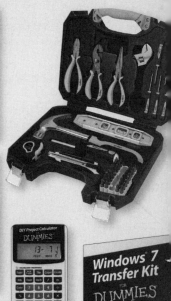